# Guide to Strategic Planning for Educators

Shirley D. McCune

Association for Supervision and Curriculum Development
Alexandria, VA

**Shirley D. McCune** is Regional Director, Mid-continent Regional Educational Laboratory, 12500 E. Iliff Ave., Suite 201, Aurora, CO 80014.

Ronald S. Brandt, Executive Editor
Nancy Carter Modrak, Manager of Publications
Fran R. Cohen, Managing Editor
Janet Frymoyer, Production Coordinator
Al Way, Art Director

Price: $6.00
ASCD Stock Number: 611-86044
ISBN: 0-87120-140-2
Library of Congress Catalog Card Number: 86-71841

Printed in the United States of America

# Contents

# Introduction

Today we find ourselves in a world of transition. The industrial age, during which the United States grew into a strong, affluent world power, is drawing to a close. A new society, the information age, continues to move powerfully into place. This transformation, first seen in the economic sector of our society, is now visible in our social, political, organizational, and personal lives.

Despite the changes evident in every sector, we are still suffering from the human problems of reorienting and reorganizing our institutions, our activities, and our lives to meet the challenges and changed conditions of our new society. History suggests that it is difficult for any civilization that excelled in one age to maintain its achievements under a new set of conditions. Our tendency is to stick with the things that worked in the past in the hope that they will eventually work again.

This is a particularly frustrating time for educational institutions. On the one hand, society is paying more attention to education's needs and beginning to provide resources aimed at improving its effectiveness. On the other hand, an awareness is slowly developing that the nature of the progress to date is unlikely to keep up with the larger changes in society. Broader questions are being raised about what is needed.

Given the changes in the larger society, what knowledge, skills, and competencies are children going to need to participate fully in the future? What should be the role of schools in meeting the larger societal needs of the present and future?

This book describes a process particularly suited to address those issues—*strategic planning*. This creative management process is powered by the basic human drive to solve problems—to eliminate discrepancies between what is and what must be. A primary value of strategic planning is that it forces people and institutions to reexamine, to refocus, and to seek out or create new means for accomplishing their purposes.

There is nothing magical about the strategic planning process, however. It takes its meaning and value from the context in which it's applied. This book, therefore, first explores that context—the economic, demographic, political, social, educational, and technological changes in the environment that already are affecting our schools.

Chapter 2 describes the strategic planning process and how it can address these conditions. The final chapter, "Strategic Management and Leadership," explores the compatibility of the strategic planning process with new forms of educational management, and its role in creating and supporting the leadership needed to address the future.

Underlying each chapter is the belief that "fixing" or improving schools in accord with outmoded images of what is possible is unlikely to push education far or fast enough. The task confronting educators and society is to *restructure* schools and to develop organizations that "match" the changing conditions of a changing society. "Restructuring" is not used here as a synonym for "improvement," although they are closely linked ends of the same process. *Improvement* focuses on bettering the state of the art, finding more effective means to relatively unchanging ends. *Restructuring*, because it is a response to changes in the external environment already affecting schools, allows for significant shifts away from what has been done in the past. It may include possibilities not derived from past experience; for example, changes in the goals of educational programs, the methods of delivering services, the clients to be served, management structures, evaluation and accountability procedures, financing, and community outreach and relationships.

The starting point for restructuring is an examination of what has changed and the identification of possibilities. Strategic planning provides an effective process for undertaking that task. It begins with an understanding of the economic, demographic, political, social, educational, and technological changes in the environment and how they affect schools. The following section outlines some of the forces affecting educational systems—forces schools must address if they are to remain productive and strong.

SHIRLEY D. McCUNE

# Chapter 1

# THE CONTEXT FOR STRATEGIC PLANNING

*"Wandering between two worlds,*
*one dead,*
*The other powerless to be born."*
*—Matthew Arnold*

## Forces Affecting Educational Systems

Change, at an ever-increasing rate, is characteristic of our society. A child entering school today comes from a world significantly different from the one that shaped many of the beliefs and assumptions of the adults who work there. Regardless of future projections, economic, demographic, and organizational changes have already taken place.

## Economic Restructuring

The United States' transformation from an industrial to an information society manifested itself first in a restructuring of the economy. John Naisbitt, author of *Megatrends*, estimates that about 60 percent of the necessary restructuring of the U.S. economy has already taken place.[1] However, the restructuring process is not over nor has it been smooth. For one thing, strong regional differences still exist in economic conditions throughout the country as well as differences in the abilities of regions to diversify and replace nonproductive activities. There is a continuing lag in anticipating and planning for change. The regional displacement and pain resulting from economic restructuring is felt unevenly throughout the country.

Following are some ways in which the U.S. economy has already been restructured:

- The nature of work has changed,
- The energy that drives society has changed,
- The United States' position in world trade has changed,
- Patterns of employment have changed, and
- The composition of the work force has changed.

Each of these economic changes has important implications for education and training. The nature of these changes and the challenges they pose for education are outlined below.

## The Nature of Work

In 1800, 80 percent of the workers in the United States held agricultural jobs; in 1984, 3 percent; and in 1986, slightly over 2 percent. This reduction of agricultural jobs continues as the farm crisis, which began in the Midwest, has expanded to other regions of the nation. Similarly, in 1950, 55 percent of United States workers held blue-collar industrial jobs; in 1984, only about 24 percent were engaged in the industrial sector.[2] Industrial jobs also continue to decline as foreign competition and automation shape our economy.

What has replaced these sectors of the economy? What has happened to the people who held these jobs? In 1980, service jobs (economic activities that do not result in tangible, storable products or require a large amount of capital or equipment) had grown to include 30 percent of all jobs.[3] (See fig. 1-1.)

Another change occurred in the number of information jobs. Information jobs are those that produce machines to handle information, run communications networks, produce new technologies, and use technologies to provide information services and products. In 1983, 56 percent of jobs in service, industry, and agriculture were classified as information jobs. Included in this category of 54 million information workers are 11 million executives and managers, 16 million professionals and technical workers, 11 million salespersons, and 16 million clerical workers.[4]

It is predicted that over the next 20 to 30 years, the number of professional and technical workers will expand from 16 to 24 percent, becoming the largest sector of the labor force. The number of clerical workers will remain proportionally stable at 15 percent, and salespeople will experience a modest increase from 11 to 15 percent.[5] On the other hand, the number of factory workers will decline 20 to 25 percent over the next decade as a result of robotic and computer-operated factory automation.[6] Twenty to 30 million of the U.S.'s 54 million white-

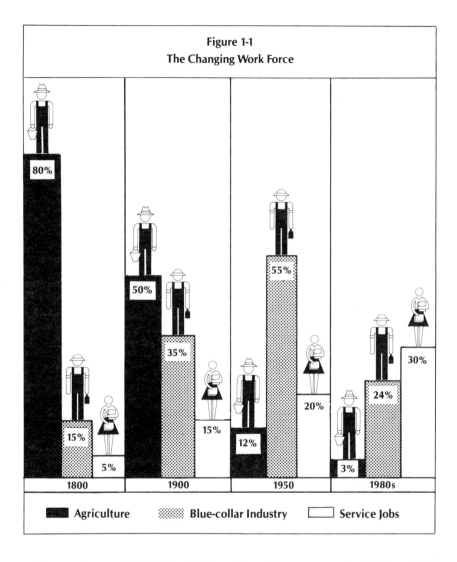

Figure 1-1
The Changing Work Force

Agriculture   Blue-collar Industry   Service Jobs

collar workers will find their jobs affected by automation before 1990, and an additional 10 million will see changes in the nature or availability of work thereafter.[7] The total number of jobs in the work force is expected to decline by perhaps 5 to 13 million positions as automation, after taking over large firms, makes inroads into smaller ones.[8]

While the number of workers will decrease, the knowledge and skills required of persons holding jobs will increase. Automation and technology demand higher abilities:

> Organizational design must recognize that information technology will totally transform traditional roles. Executives will be upgraded from

investors to planners. Managers will be upgraded from coordinators to investors. Professional and technical personnel will be upgraded from specialists to generalists engaged in organizing the delivery of services to customers. Clerical personnel will be upgraded from support-staff members to specialists in the delivery of information services. Salespersons will be upgraded from distributors of information to general managers of customer care and retention.[9]

The primary outcome of this restructuring is in the nature of work itself. In the past, physical capabilities and specialized skills were the essentials for employment. But work today and in the future is increasingly a matter of an individual's intellectual skills—the ability to process and use information. Information workers will be required to have even higher levels of literacy and thinking skills to find and hold jobs.

Not only will future workers need to possess higher levels of literacy and thinking, they will be required to continually upgrade their knowledge and skills. It is estimated that a majority of jobs in the future will be substantially restructured every five to seven years. Work itself will include a significant amount of learning and the development of new knowledge. Future projections suggest that employers should budget as much as 25 percent of their labor costs for the education and training of professional and technical workers.[10]

Shifts in the use of information as key elements of work have created an inextricable dependency between knowledge and the economic activities of our society. Knowledge creates new goods and services, improves production and manufacturing procedures, and results in better management and organizational strategies. Future increases in productivity and economic growth are closely linked to quantitative and qualitative increases in the nation's educational and training systems. It is estimated that two-thirds of the increases in productivity are the results of human resources while capital resources account for about one-third of the input components.[11] The nation's ability to recognize this and restructure educational and training systems will determine, in large measure, our economic and social well-being.

### The Power that Drives Society

The power sources of a society not only determine the nature of production and productivity but also shape societal development. The agricultural era of American society was organized around the use of human and animal power and the natural energies of wind, sun, and water. These power sources were comparatively inefficient, uncontrolled, and undependable. The physical strength of a man was often the most important consideration in his getting and holding a job.

The transition of the United States from an agricultural to an industrial society was made possible by the development of machinery and technologies. The invention of the steam engine and gasoline motor, and the generation of electricity, made possible a society where human and animal power could be replaced by machines fueled by coal and oil. These became the primary power sources. They opened the door to mass production systems that could produce goods more efficiently than ever imagined. The effect was, indeed, revolutionary.

Today, another revolution is in the making. The development of the microprocessor has made possible new breakthroughs in the use of information. The storage or communication of information using such devices as the telephone, telegraph, radio, television, movies, and so on, had already increased the speed of information transmission, the quality of information, and the distribution of information. What was missing, however, was a readily available way to process, analyze, and store information. The microchip provided an effective, efficient, and relatively inexpensive method of handling large quantities of information. Information thus became a major power for developing products and technologies.

Although science and technological developments played a role in American life for over a century, it was the success of science and technology in World War II that stimulated a national policy to promote scientific research and development. This policy brought forth a period of remarkable growth in scientific knowledge and led to advances in a wide range of technologies.[12] The scientific background and experience created an infrastructure waiting for breakthroughs in more effective ways of conducting research and handling information. The microchip provided this power or spark—the needed breakthrough for developments in science and technology.

Seven technologies that are shaping and will continue to shape the U.S. economy and society are microelectronics, biogenetics, robotics, lasers, fiber optics, solar exploration, and undersea mining. The incredible progress in these areas has been made possible, in large measure, by the ability the microchip has given us to process large amounts of data efficiently and inexpensively.

Microprocessors have become an essential element of scientific and technological progress. Incredibly, their influence is felt in nearly every area of our lives. In the workplace, information tools are changing the nature of work itself, the structure of organizations, the relationship of employees to organizations and their work, and the type of products and services produced. Microprocessors are becoming commonplace in the home as control devices for domestic appliances, as tools for personnel and management, as extensions of other communications technologies, and as vehicles for education and training.

For the two decades following World War II, the United States dominated worldwide scientific and technological research and development. Since then, as other countries have made strides in research and technology, the position of the United States has declined. Today America conducts roughly over one-third of the world's total basic research with the remainder divided equally between Western Europe and Japan on one side, and the nations of the Soviet bloc on the other.[13] To a large extent, the microchip has made possible the rapid development of other countries.

It is apparent that maintaining a strong position in science and technology is essential to our future well-being. Technology has been one of America's key exports and contributions to the world. Not only must we continue to develop scientifically and technologically, we must also use the knowledge we gain to help educate the literate and skilled populations essential to our future.

While U.S. scientists are among the best in the world, many Americans are mathematically and scientifically illiterate. International comparisons demonstrate that American students lag behind students in most countries tested. A University of Michigan study suggests, "not only does American achievement lag behind that of children in Japan and Taiwan, but it does so virtually from the first day they enter school."[14]

The power of the microchip must be applied not only in science, technology, and economic development, but also to extend the knowledge and skills of our people. Developing human capital is critical if we are to maintain a strong economy and position within the world community.

### The U.S. Position in World Trade

The United States economy has grown from a national to a global one. World trade, which comprised 6 percent of the U.S. Gross National Product (GNP) in the early 1960s accounted for 15 percent of the GNP in the early 1980s. However, the United States' share of world trade is declining—in 1980 it was 11 percent, down from 20 percent in 1950 (fig. 1-2).[15]

United States exports declined from $38.2 billion in 1981 to $21.9 billion in 1983, a reduction estimated to have cost us 25,000 jobs. As exports declined, imports increased by 10.9 percent between 1981 and 1983. Imported goods now account for 19 percent of American consumption, up from 9 percent in 1970. This trade imbalance of exports and imports resulted in a deficit of nearly $150 billion in 1985.[16]

While many reasons are cited for this trade imbalance (the value of the U.S. dollar, debts of other countries, etc.), the primary factor is our standard of living and the wages of U.S. workers compared to

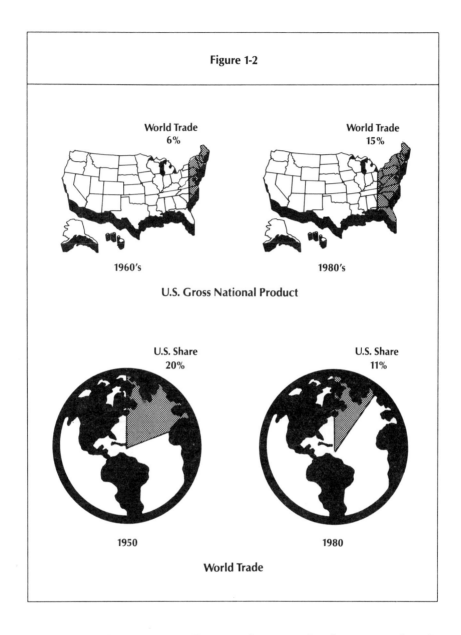

Figure 1-2

World Trade
6%

World Trade
15%

1960's

1980's

U.S. Gross National Product

U.S. Share
20%

U.S. Share
11%

1950

1980

World Trade

workers in other countries. In 1983, for example, the average hourly wage for auto workers in the U.S. was $19.07, while in Japan it was $7.91.

In the past we viewed Japan as our chief competitor. Today, however, we find Korea and a host of other countries producing goods at much lower costs than possible in the United States or Japan. Korean workers, for example, work 7 days a week (with 2 days off a year), 12 hours a day, to produce home video recorders sold in the U.S. They earn only $3,000 a year.[17] Obviously, American producers cannot compete with these labor costs. We must find other ways to be more productive.

An optimist's global strategy once envisioned a worldwide assembly line with the U.S. supplying knowledge and technology, the other countries providing low-wage, low-skilled labor. Other countries, especially Japan, are beginning to realize that their future also depends on the production of knowledge and technology for countries with lower labor costs, and they are moving into many areas the United States once dominated.

If the U.S. wants to compete, one undesirable alternative is to lower the standard of living of its low-skilled workers. A more realistic alternative, however, is to train highly skilled and educated workers and support them with the best technologies. The lead time required for this people investment is considerable, making immediate action essential.

Yet another cause for our declining balance of trade is our general neglect of international issues and perspectives. Although most Americans understand the importance of a strong military defense and the foreign policies underlying world peace, many are woefully uninformed about the geography, history, and culture of other countries. U.S. students must be prepared to live and think in terms of a global economy and understand the need for cultural exchange and trade with other countries. They must learn to view situations within a context of history and culture different from our own. Curriculum should include a second language for all students, world history, world geography, and a grasp of culture as a primary framework for analyzing all areas of knowledge.

## Patterns of Employment

Relatively stable in the 1950s and 1960s, the U.S. economy underwent a recession beginning in the mid-1970s and then moved into a short-term recovery in the 1980s. Continued economic growth is projected, although at a slower rate than in the past. This "shakedown" of the economy has created patterns of change that represent significant deviations from the past.

Perhaps one of the most important changes has been the growth of entrepreneurial small businesses. An estimated 640,000 new businesses started up in 1984, outnumbering business closures 20 to 1.[18] This may be compared to an estimated 50,000 businesses started in 1980.

This growth of small to medium-sized businesses has been prompted by several factors: technological changes that do not require extensive capital outlays; the rise of the service industry, which also does not require extensive capital; and the targeting of specialized markets. Finally, more and more people desire to be autonomous and to work for themselves.

These businesses offer new services and products as well as jobs for many. Over time, however, they have a high rate of failure. This points to the need for preparing our population with a better understanding of the business world and knowledge of the skills and competencies required to manage businesses.

A second trend in the employment sphere is the polarization of jobs into highly skilled/high pay and low skilled/low pay. Jobs requiring middle-level skills for middle-level pay are scarce due to production cutbacks in the steel and automotive industries, the wider use of automation to perform supervisory and mid-management tracking functions, and a general upgrading of jobs without a commensurate increase in salaries.

Unemployment levels in the 1980s rose from 6 to 9 percent with a current stabilization at approximately 7 percent. This rate has been reduced somewhat by growing numbers of part-time employees. While some part-time employment may be a sign of worker preference, a good deal results from lack of full-time jobs.

Unemployment affects minorities and women disproportionately. In 1980, the unemployment rate for black males was 12.4 percent; for black females, 11.9 percent; for white males, 5.3 percent; and for white females, 5.6 percent.[19] Disproportionate unemployment rates result from discrimination, inadequate training and skills, plus a host of related social problems such as transportation, child care, access to training, and so on.

Although efforts in the 1960s and 1970s to overcome race and sex discrimination resulted in significant progress for many Americans, the outlook is discouraging. Conflicts regarding enforcement of civil rights laws, continuing underrepresentation of minorities in science and technology programs, the decline of minorities enrolled in college, and societal stereotyping continue to limit opportunities for a significant portion of the population.

### Composition of the Work Force

The large-scale entry of women into the paid work force is one of the most significant changes of this century. In 1982, 53 percent of American women were employed, compared to 38 percent of all women in 1960. The most recent entrants to the work force have been women with children under six. Whereas 28 percent of women with children

9

under six worked in 1970, 45 percent of these women were working in 1982.[20] (See fig. 1-3.)

Approximately seven of ten women work due to economic necessity. Of the 37 million women who work, 8.5 million are single; 6.9 million are widowed, divorced, or separated; and 9.5 million are married to husbands earning less than $10,000 a year.[21]

Despite growing numbers of women in the work force, women are unlikely to soon command salaries comparable to those of men. Women currently earn 61 cents for every dollar earned by men, down from 64 cents in 1955. In 1984, on the average, a female college graduate earned $2,000 a year less than a man who had completed only high school.[22] Efforts continue for women to gain equal pay for work of equal value.

The reasons for inequitable pay vary. One is that women are concentrated in sex-segregated low-paying professions. Differences in education, age, and years of experience also contribute to the overall pattern of inequity. But even in studies where these variables are held constant, women are consistently paid less. For example, women's pay in administrative and managerial fields is only 52 percent of male earnings.[23] A certain amount of this differential must be attributed to sex discrimination.

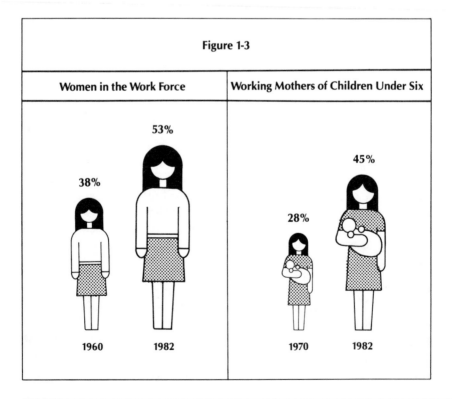

Figure 1-3

| Women in the Work Force | Working Mothers of Children Under Six |
|---|---|

Greater numbers of minority workers are also entering the work force. Currently, minorities make up 13 percent of the work force. This number is expected to expand to over 14 percent by 1995, based on the higher birth rate in the minority community and a higher immigration rate among youth.[24]

Like women, minorities face discrimination in job and pay. Providing minority youth with the necessary knowledge and skills for participation in the work force is also a problem. In 1985 the high school dropout rate for white students was 14 percent, in contrast to 24 percent of black students and 40 percent of Hispanics.[25]

Another change in the work force is the growing number of older workers. Although the Baby Boom generation has the education and experience, these workers must deal with increased competition for advancement and future pressures to make room for younger workers. Baby Boomers must confront efforts to pressure them into early retirement, alternative positions, or taking sabbaticals and so on. The nation will be challenged to find ways to use the skills of older persons no longer in the work force.

## Challenges for Education

A review of economic changes may, at first glance, seem removed from the educational world. Yet the future of the U.S. economy will be influenced profoundly by the response of the educational community. The shift from an industrial to an information society places the importance of educational and training systems in a new light as the ability to develop, analyze, and apply information becomes the primary activity of this society. Education and training systems, and the institutions that develop them, will be the critical human infrastructure of our society.

Education and training will occupy positions of greater importance in our society. Education is projected to surpass medicine and health care, becoming the largest industry in America.[26] Thus educational expenditures are likely to increase dramatically. Some predict that the total annual expenditures for education will grow 20 to 25 percent between 1981 and 1990. These increases will be needed to educate the children of the baby boomers ($8–10 billion between 1981 and 1990), retrain midcareer employees ($60–150 billion), retrain technologically displaced workers ($45–120 billion), and retrain workers to use new technologies ($400–500 billion). This will necessitate an average yearly increase of $73–110 billion between 1984 and 1990.

The restructuring of our economy will change the role of education and training systems from programs for socializing youth and adults to institutions essential to economic survival and well-being. This shift requires the type of reexamination of public policy and past assumptions that strategic planning makes possible.

To solve problems we must discard old assumptions and structures. Meeting our new needs may require new patterns of collaboration and work among government and private and public agencies. It may also force us to examine basic values such as the degree to which education and training are public, private, or employer responsibilities and how resources should be obtained to meet educational and training needs. New forms of service delivery, financing, and responsibility are likely to surface.

Strategic planning provides a process for examining possibilities. It leads us to new levels of openness and understanding essential for inventing new approaches to meet society's changing needs.

# Demographic Shifts

People are the most important resource of any nation. The characteristics of a nation's population shape that nation's destiny. Most people have some awareness that the U.S. population is changing—we are experiencing a "graying" or an aging of Americans, racial-ethnic minorities are increasing, family structures have changed, and children have become the poorest group within the population. Although we may have heard these statistics, the implications probably have not been fully considered by individuals or by the educational, social, or economic institutions that will be forced to deal with these changes. Some of the changes in our population and their implications for schools are discussed below.

### Age: The Graying of America

It was 1946. World War II was over for Americans, and a sense of urgency and a need to get things back to normal prevailed. "Normal" included having children and raising families. This spirit, highlighting as it did the importance of home and family, paved the way to a population increase so widespread that it was labeled America's "Baby Boom." In 1957, at the height of the Baby Boom, American women were having children at the rate of 3.7 per lifetime.[27] The Baby Boom lasted from 1946 to 1964 and brought with it a host of social and economic problems. Home and school buildings couldn't keep pace with the demand, maternity wards and child health resources were strained, and the pattern of suburbia as a place to raise children became an American way of life.

The generation of Baby Boomers was to transform American culture. Parents who had lived through the Great Depression yearned for more for their children. The youth culture became a part of the American scene as the Baby Boomers made their mark on the educational, social, and economic institutions of our society.

Society was still struggling with the impact of the Baby Boom when the U.S. birth rate fell to 1.27 and we entered the years of the Baby Bust from 1964 to 1978. The Baby Bust was a time to breathe, but not for long. We soon faced the problems of school closings because of fewer students.

When the Baby Boomers approached child-rearing age, they tended to postpone having children, so the full impact of the adult Baby Boomers was not felt until 1978 when we began to experience an "Echo Baby Boom." (See fig. 1-4.) Due to population increases, the actual number of babies is comparable to the 1950s although the birth rate is much lower. Today, the birth rate for American women is 1.87 per lifetime. Of course, the rate differs considerably by race (e.g., fertility for white women is 1.7; for black women, 2.4; and 2.9 for Mexican-American women).[28]

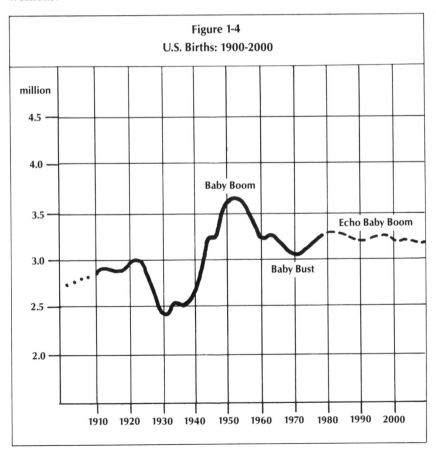

Figure 1-4
U.S. Births: 1900-2000

Birth patterns have given rise to two population groupings—the larger number of Baby Boomers who are middle-aged, midcareer, and largely white; and a second group of young children who increasingly represent the offspring of minority groups. One set of concerns for the larger society will be about caring for the needs of older citizens. A second set of concerns will be about dealing with the needs of growing numbers of children and providing for them as they grow to adulthood.

Most of the Baby Boomers will be retired by 2020, the cost of their retirement being provided in part by the smaller number of Baby Bust workers. Planning and caring for the demands of this ever-expanding age group, which is likely to live longer and longer due to improvements in health and medicine, is an awesome prospect. In 1950 for example, 17 workers supported each person receiving Social Security retirement benefits. By 1992, only three workers will support each retiree, and one of the three will belong to a minority group (fig. 1-5).[29]

Growth in educational services will be necessary as increased numbers of children enter elementary schools in the areas where young families are locating. This is also true considering the number of people enrolling in adult and continuing education courses.

### Racial-Ethnic Factors

The heterogeneity of the U.S. population has increased and will continue to increase. Of the 240 million people in the United States, about 50 million (21 percent) are racial-ethnic minorities. Although minorities make up 21 percent of the total population, nearly 28 percent of the total public school population belong to a minority group.

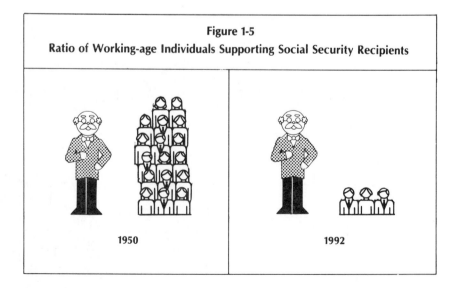

**Figure 1-5**
**Ratio of Working-age Individuals Supporting Social Security Recipients**

1950

1992

Today, the average white American is 31 years old, the average black American is 25, and the average Hispanic American is only 23.[30] White Americans are moving out of their child-bearing years just as minority Americans are moving into them. The population of minority children will continue to increase in the future, and these numbers will be further increased by immigration. About 40 percent of legal immigrants come from Asia, and another 40 percent come from Mexico and Central and South America. Three-fourths of illegal immigrants come from Mexico and Central and South America. The largest number of immigrants (57,557 in 1984) came from Mexico, followed by the Philippines (42,767), Vietnam (37,236), Korea (33,042), India (24,964), China (23,363), and the Dominican Republic (23,147).[31] The trend of European immigration has been replaced with a new trend dominated by Hispanic and Asian immigrants.

Increases in the school enrollments of minorities are evident in many areas of the country, but the bulk is concentrated in a group of states that starts in New York, moves southward down the Atlantic coast, and then westward ending in California. Black school enrollment is highest in the District of Columbia, Mississippi, South Carolina, Alabama, and Georgia; Hispanic enrollment is highest in New Mexico, Texas, California, and Arizona.

Three of our largest states—California, Texas, and Florida—are nearing a majority of minority students. More than 50 percent of California's elementary school students belong to minority groups, 46 percent of Texas' students are black or Hispanic, and 32.2 percent of Florida's students are minority Americans.

Minorities also tend to concentrate in urban areas, and these concentrations have swelled because of immigrant resettlement. Large numbers of immigrants continue to settle in New York City, Los Angeles, Chicago, San Francisco, Anaheim, Miami, and Washington, D.C. In the 25 largest school systems in the nation, a majority of the students come from minority groups.[32]

Increases in the percentages of minority students create significant problems for schools. Working with heterogeneous groups of students is invariably more complex and difficult. What this means for minority students is lower levels of achievement, a higher dropout level, and a general lower level of achievement of those skills that prepare one for life. For example, while the national dropout rate is 28 percent, within urban centers such as New York, Philadelphia, and Chicago, over 45 percent of high school students drop out.[33]

Why this discrepancy in academic success? The reasons are many. Teachers and staff may expect less from minority and low-income children. Teaching methods may not be sufficiently varied to meet the needs of heterogeneous populations. The curriculum may be irrelevant to the lives of minority children. Resources for schools with high concentrations of low-income and minority children are likely to be inadequate. Necessary special services such as bilingual education, remediation, individualized instruction, counseling, and so on may be nonexistent or limited.

Failure in school among minority youth poses a threat to the future of the nation. As literacy requirements for participation in the larger society increase, lack of academic achievement condemns minorities and low-income children to limited futures, lessening the quality of life and benefits from society they can expect. In addition, the future social costs of undereducated youth in terms of crime, welfare, and lost economic productivity emphasize the immediate need for action to improve educational achievement. Finally, the diversity that has made America great is threatened. Each cultural group possesses unique information and insights. The blending of this information is essential for a future democratic society.

## Family Patterns

In 1955, the Dick and Jane family—with father working outside the home, a mother working in the home, and two or more children—was the norm and basic model of family life. This picture described nearly 60 percent of the nation's families at that time. By 1980, only 11 percent of families fit this pattern, and today, only 4 percent (fig. 1-6).[34]

America's 80 million households and families are diversifying as family patterns increasingly include two working parents with children, childless couples (26 million as compared to 24 million married couples with children), single-parent families (10 million), individuals living alone (20 million), and other variations.[35]

A major reason for the change in American family life can be traced to increasing divorce rates. In 1960, 393,000 American couples were divorced; by 1985 that number had increased to 1,187,000.[36] Today, one out of every two marriages ends in divorce. This increase has changed the economic, social, and psychological positions of women and children. In most cases of divorce, women end up with the children and the responsibility for supporting them. As a result, an ex-wife's disposable income is likely to fall by 73 percent in the year following divorce, while her ex-husband's rises by 42 percent.[37] The rise in child poverty thus can be accounted for in part by increasing divorce rates and the restructuring of family income.

While most children continue to live with two parents, this number is decreasing rapidly. Only 4 of 10 children born in 1983 (41 percent) will live with both parents until they reach 18.[38]

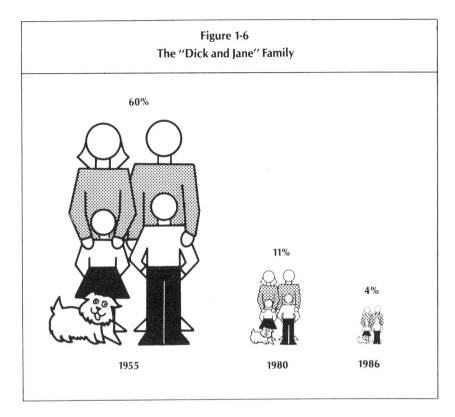

**Figure 1-6**
**The "Dick and Jane" Family**

In 1983, 23 percent of all children lived in single-parent families. In 91 percent of them, the head of the household was female. More than 50 percent of all black children lived in single-parent families, compared with 25 percent of Hispanic children and 16 percent of white children.[39]

An equally important trend in American life is the teenage mother. Four out of every ten adolescent females will become pregnant; two will have abortions, and two will give birth. In 1983, women under 20 had 14 percent (nearly 500,000) of all births. More than half of these mothers were unmarried, and the vast majority of the one million pregnancies were unplanned.[40]

Although blacks make up only about 15 percent of the teenage population, half of the births in 1983 were to black mothers. Black teenage girls are much more likely to give birth than white girls. The birth rate for black teenage girls has declined, however, and a corresponding increase has occurred among white teenage girls.

If a teenage girl gives birth, there is a 30 percent chance that she will have a second or third child. Every day 40 teenagers give birth to their third child. Forty-three percent of female school dropouts do so because of pregnancy or marriage. Half of the teenage mothers drop out of school never to return.[41]

Trends in family patterns suggest that the stability and the resources provided by two-parent families can no longer be considered the norm for children. This places pressures on the children, the families, and the institutions that serve them. Children from single-parent families reportedly have more discipline problems in school and lower academic achievement. While this seems natural given the increased support that a two-parent family provides, schools must recognize the problems facing single-parent children and make an effort to provide interpersonal support as an integral part of the learning process.

## Sex Roles

Changes in family patterns are inextricably linked with changes in the roles of women and men in our society. Perhaps one of the most important social changes in this century has been the movement of women into the paid work force. At the beginning of the century, less than 20 percent of women worked outside the home. Today, 53 percent of all women over 18 are in the paid work force, and 53 percent of all married women work outside the home.[42]

Despite women's increased participation, they have been unable to command the salary of men. Women currently make only 61 cents for every dollar that men earn. This inequality of earning power becomes especially important when we understand that women increasingly have shouldered the responsibility for the support of children. Divorce, lower wages, and limited services create a situation wherein more and more women and children live below the poverty line. In 1984 nearly 25 percent of all children lived in poverty.[43] In urban areas the percentage is much higher. For example, 40 percent of all children in New York City live in poverty.[44] Before 1974 the majority of the poor in America were older citizens. The majority of poor in America are now children. Fifty-six percent of the children living in households headed by women are poor.[45]

There are dramatic differences in childhood poverty among racial-ethnic groups. A black child is about three times as likely as a white child to be born into poverty; a Hispanic child is more than twice as likely to be poor. Sixty-nine percent of black families headed by women are living in poverty, whereas 23 percent of two-parent black families are poor. Figures on childhood poverty by age and race are provided in Figure 1-7.[46] It is important to remember that numerically the largest group of poor is white, even though poverty rates vary significantly among racial-ethnic groups.

If we are to change the economic future of these children, we must look to education as the means of developing the knowledge and skills

| Figure 1-7 Children in Poverty by Age and Race, 1983 | | | |
|---|---|---|---|
| Age | White | Black | Hispanic |
| Total, all ages | 12.1 | 35.7 | 28.4 |
| Under 15 years | 18.1 | 47.6 | 39.0 |
| 15 to 17 years | 13.9 | 42.6 | 34.0 |
| 18 to 21 years | 13.7 | 39.6 | 28.0 |

*U.S. Bureau of the Census.*

that will prepare them for productive adult lives. Schools must recognize the special needs of disadvantaged children and give them what they need for academic success. Given the increasing number of minority children, the importance of this task cannot be overemphasized. Society will require citizens with high levels of knowledge and skill. Minority students continue to lag behind white students on measures of academic performance. Although progress has been made, black and Hispanic students tend to score far below their white peers on standardized tests. While effective schools research demonstrates that this gap can be reduced, communities and schools commit themselves to ensuring that all children will be adequately prepared for a future society.

## Challenges for Education

The changing demographics of our nation have created our current problems and herald more difficult ones in the future. A democratic society is built on the assumption of equal opportunity for all. Reversing the trend toward ever-larger inequities among groups calls for renewed and expanded efforts of the larger community and many institutions. Schools remain the key institutions for responding to the needs of people and building the types of communities that are essential to our future survival and well-being.

The changing demographics of our society will require important changes in our schools, including:

• *Expanding programs of early childhood development.* Early childhood is a critical developmental time during which a child's self-concept and framework for intellectual and social abilities are established. The child's general language skills are formed, and social development skills emerge. A major longitudinal study of disadvantaged children cited the value of preschool experiences because of a "chain of cause and effect."[47] Preschool provides increased intellectual and social competence, giving children a head start in first grade. Students with preschool experience demonstrate higher scholastic achievement, are more likely to graduate from high school, less likely to engage in crime, more likely to be employed as young adults, less likely to go on welfare, and less likely to become teenage mothers.

The study concluded that the investment in early childhood education is beneficial. The savings that accrue to society from less crime, welfare, and other costs were seven times the cost of one year of preschool and three-and-one-half times the cost of two years of preschool.

Early childhood education is critical for the disadvantaged and desirable for middle-class children. Intellectual and social skills gained during this experience benefit all children. Preschool also provides parents with needed child care during the day. They continue to grow in popularity as more working mothers decide to work and pursue careers.

Preschool programs provide a natural extension of public school services. Schools are usually located in communities where such services are needed. Preschool programs may be provided free, or there may be a fee. As the need for such programs increases, schools should examine what is taught in preschool and how to head off academic problems that might appear later on.

• *Child support services.* A large variety of child support services are useful to all children, but especially to disadvantaged children. These vary from programs that focus on extended educational activities to those that provide before- and after-school activities for children of working parents (latch-key programs), newcomer center programs for children of recent immigrants, expanded learning programs for students in need of assistance, programs for gifted children, and alternative education programs. Other programs may deal with dependency, child health, and nutrition, and may be offered in collaboration with other community agencies and groups.

• *A variety of learning methods.* The increasing heterogeneity of school children has had a profound impact on curriculum and instructional concerns. Curriculum should include content that is relevant to the lives of children. Instruction should reflect the needs of a diverse population with differing learning styles. Increasing the variety of learning methods in the classroom can improve student learning for all groups.

• *Options for secondary students.* While definitive studies are not available, a preliminary study suggests that the movement for higher standards for high school graduation appears to help good students (those already getting As and Bs) improve their scores on standardized tests and probably their general levels of learning. Students with lower grades do not show similar improvement in test performance or in levels of learning.[48] Another study suggested that recommendations for a more structured curriculum might lead to less student choice and greater student stratification, resulting in more student failure.[49]

These effects may be overcome by providing more options for students in terms of curriculum content and school size, structure, and climate. The assumption that a single "tough" curriculum will meet the needs of all students does not correspond with what we know about the levels of diversity among students. Having a variety of program options is especially important for secondary students.

• *Multicultural education.* Multicultural education programs in schools are not new, but most are based on a comparatively limited definition of culture. Typically, multicultural programs focus on human relations, intergroup relations, and some understanding of other cultures within the American experience. Important as this approach may be, cultural similarities and differences should be the framework used throughout the curriculum.

Culture may be defined as any way a group does things. Helping children understand global cultures, the reasons behind cultural mores and decisions, and the ways cultural differences affect international relations are essential to prepare them for an increasingly diverse society and world.

• *Educational services for adults.* The need for education is not limited to children. Adult educational needs run the gamut from basic skills, job training, and personal growth to individual interests. Some schools are responding to these needs and extending adult education programs. Examples include parenting programs, job training, and personal counseling.

Changed demographics in our society present a new set of challenges for schools. If schools ignore these challenges they will be met by other agencies, thereby weakening the schools' position. On the other hand, the challenges can be seen as opportunities for strengthening the educational system and the schools' position in the community. It would be naive to assume that all districts will welcome the changed demographics and find positive ways to deal with such problems as greater age diversity, racial-ethnic diversity, and changed family patterns and sex roles. We can safely assume, however, that those schools that meet this challenge will ensure not only their own but also their community's survival.

## Organizational Changes

A third set of forces that shapes education is the changing structure of organizations such as government, business, and industry. These changes, largely the result of changing technology and economics, will inevitably affect educational institutions. Some manifestations of these changes are already evident in education, and they parallel structural changes already observed in other sectors of society. A number of changes could be identified, but the four that seem most relevant to education are the decentralization of organizations, high tech-high touch, multiple options, and participation. Each of these is discussed below.

### The Decentralization of Organizations

The decentralization of government, business, and unions is a hallmark of the information society. Until World War II American organizations were patterned toward bigness—big business, big government, and big unions—but a reversal of this pattern was evident as early as the 1950s as organizations began to decentralize.

Decentralization has increased significantly during the past ten years. Many government decisions have shifted from federal to state agencies and, in some instances, from state to local agencies. Corporations have "flattened" their management structures, delegating more tasks to lower levels and requiring more employees to manage themselves. Many large corporations have found ways to organize work around self-contained but interdependent units that give people a greater sense of belonging and identity. The lesson of size is that small seems to be better for producing effective and efficient organizations.

Decentralization is taking place in education in a variety of ways. State educational policies have replaced federal programs and policies. Local policy and decision makers become increasingly important as decentralization of programs and decisions begins to move from state to local levels.

A second manifestation of decentralization is the reduction in the number of extremely large schools. Schools with more than 1,800 secondary or 600 elementary students are no longer desirable. There is definitely a trend toward smaller schools with more positive learning climates.

Another example is the decentralization from the district to the building level. This development, known as school-based management, grew out of the effective schools research, which highlighted the importance of building management in developing a supportive climate for learning. The goal of school-based management is to let those people make decisions who will carry them out, thereby providing building principals with greater autonomy and freedom. This does not imply a less important or active role for the district. On the contrary, it requires an even better district structure and operation, with the district providing direction and resources for schools.

The application of school-based management is an example of "tight-loose" principles identified by Peters and Waterman in *In Search of Excellence.*[50] The structural systems of the district (physical facilities, personnel, budget, transportation, etc.) and the district program systems (goals, curriculum, instruction, assessment, staff development, etc.) must be "tight" so that they will provide direction, goals, expectations, and standards for evaluation. Building staff must decide how to accomplish these goals; the methods of goal attainment are "loose." District goals provide an umbrella or structure for schools while simultaneously offering flexibility for building goals and approaches. Excellent schools require effective district and building management systems and a strong linkage between these two levels. Administrators must understand the similarities and differences in the management of systems (central staff) and programs (building staff).

### High Tech—High Touch

Many changes in management systems are the result of technologies that make possible new forms of organization. The basic principle is that whenever new technology is introduced to an organization, there will be a counterbalancing human response. The impersonal use of technology creates the need for and makes possible a greater emphasis on high-touch activities. Large companies with thousands of employees are able to keep track of employees and develop individual work and benefit plans by using computers and other data processing technologies.

As technology is introduced to increase the productivity of classrooms, schools, or districts, there will be a need for compensating high-touch efforts. For example, classroom use of technology can free the teacher from the responsibility of delivering some of the content, thus making time for more interaction with and individualized attention to students.

The use of technology in management can reduce or eliminate data handling and processing time and free managers for more people-oriented activities. The synthesis of technology with educational tasks opens new possibilities for more humanistic schools and educational systems. It isn't high tech *or* high touch, but high tech and high touch working together to improve productivity and the quality of work and learning.

### Multiple Options

The ever-increasing diversity of the U.S. population and the use of information technologies for marketing have spawned demands for a wide range of products and services. Today's successful businesses have to make decisions about the quality of the products they will sell (ranging from discount stores to boutiques), the clients they wish to attract (their age levels and socioeconomic status), and the degree of service they wish to provide (ranging from self-service to personalized service).

The same demand may be seen in the field of education. Parents and children have different educational goals and preferences. Districts that recognize and respond to these differences by offering multiple options (alternative schools or programs, magnet schools, etc.) have laid the foundation for broader community support. Even when alternative schools or programs are not feasible, efforts should be made to encourage differences among school programs. Educational excellence is the result of building on the unique resources of a school (staff interests, student interests, community resources) rather than attempting to impose a uniform approach on each school.

Districts that do not respond to the demand for multiple options are likely to find themselves in competition with private schools or other groups. If public schools do not meet the desires of the community, dissatisfied parents and students will find schools or programs that will.


## Participation

Worker involvement in structuring tasks and activities has long been recognized as a means of improving morale and productivity. If information workers are expected to carry out a broader range of tasks, they must be involved in meaningful ways—to understand the larger context of their work, to participate in making decisions that affect them, and to help create a sense of culture for the total organization. This requires a different balance of power and responsibility between manager and employee than the traditional manager/assembly-line worker relationship. Information workers must retain significant independence and responsibility for planning and implementing work. Managers should provide the structure (sense of direction), resources, and oversight to ensure organizational accountability. Often work is carried out in small groups in a collegial fashion. This is a far cry from the older style of "get-go" management where workers got their orders and jumped to carry them out.

We are just beginning to find ways to make this happen in schools. Participative management with strong contacts between the superintendent, central office staff, and principals builds a framework for the systems of the district. The principal must, in turn, make contact and build relationships with teachers to ensure successful program development and delivery. The best way to build strong educational programs and cultures is to increase worker participation at all levels.

To extend this participation we must develop a common under-standing and philosophy that pervades district activities. This is not simply a matter of handing out sheets of paper. The philosophy must be modeled by persons in the system, and it must be articulated and discussed. The daily behavior of leaders, the style of supervisory ac-tivities, staff development programs, and rewards and reinforcements can help managers foster participation and develop positive learning cultures.

## Challenges for Education

Changes in organizational structures and characteristics are the third set of forces to which schools and educational institutions must respond. Some implications of these organizational changes are:

• *The need for new structures in district and school organization and management.* Decentralizing programs or moving to school-based management is likely to succeed to the degree that overall district systems (mission, goals, curriculum, instruction, staff development, facilities, budget, etc.) are in place and district and building goals can be coupled or coordinated. The basic function of the district is to identify what is to be done, and the basic task of the building is to decide how it is to be accomplished.

Developing these structures is a dynamic process usually requiring progressive stages of planning and implementation. We can use im-provement planning, strategic planning, and organizational change programs to put effective and efficient structures and procedures in place.

• *New methods of work.* The use of various technologies can lead to increased productivity in terms of student learning, administrative efficiency, and classroom management. Finding resources to acquire the hardware and train the staff to incorporate them into their work activities are important management tasks.

Technologies can open up new types of programming. They can give rural schools access to courses and learning resources never before available. Students can carry out research, simulations, and other forms of analysis that enhance learning. Computers, videotapes, video discs, and other technologies may be used in nearly every subject area for any number of purposes.

• *Building a learning culture.* A positive school climate with an open and caring staff is essential for quality education. Building and maintaining this culture is a primary management task. Participation and openness on the part of management is an essential component of positive learning cultures.

Skill at promoting participation requires knowing what to involve staff members in and how to do so. For example, asking teachers what food they would like to have at the district picnic may help in planning the picnic, but it is no substitute for involving teachers in the core activities of curriculum and instruction. Staff members would participate in making decisions that will affect their work. Needless to say, staff involvement does not necessarily mean that all ideas will be adopted, but it does give people the opportunity to express their opinions.

## The Direction of Change

The three sets of forces outlined in the previous section place strong pressures on schools to not only improve what they are doing now, but also to restructure their goals, programs, delivery systems, staff roles, evaluation systems, outreach activities, and financing. Directions for this restructuring will vary from community to community, but each will face changes that require responses. (It is impossible to specify all of the directions for restructuring schools, but some are outlined and discussed in Appendix A.)

Restructuring calls for a fundamental examination of changes in the larger society and for a process for making decisions about the desired future of schools. Change creates opportunities at the same time as it poses threats to an organization. Schools must realize that it will be impossible to maintain the status quo when powerful forces are pushing for higher levels of education.

## The Stages of School Evolution

How can schools respond? Where should they begin? Today, as we observe districts across the nation, we see a process of evolution as schools begin to mobilize themselves to meet changed and changing conditions. Figure 1-8 outlines the pattern of evolution and change.

Stage 1 describes the industrial, smokestack school that was designed to meet the needs of an industrial age. The factory served as a model for schools during this period, and it is possible to see traces of teaching methods designed to prepare most students for dull, repetitive work. Schools at this stage are often unaware of world changes as they continue to prepare students for a lost society.

Stage 2 addresses schools that realize things are not quite right and are concerned about bringing themselves "up to snuff." Literature on effective schools and effective teaching frequently guides their improvement efforts. Questions confronted by these schools are: "What should we be doing?" and "How should we be doing it?" Such questions focus on the effectiveness of schools ("Are we doing the right things?") and their efficiency ("Are we doing things right?"). In a sense this

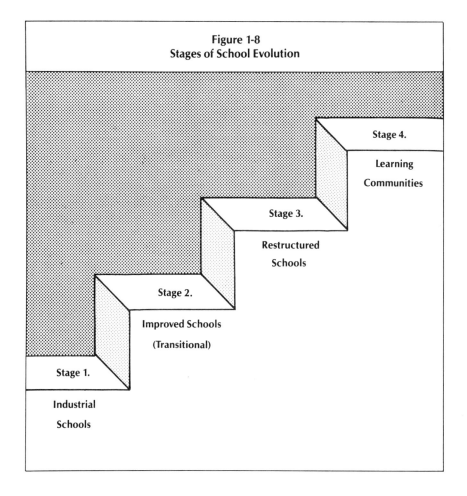

**Figure 1-8**
**Stages of School Evolution**

Stage 4.

Learning
Communities

Stage 3.

Restructured
Schools

Stage 2.

Improved Schools
(Transitional)

Stage 1.

Industrial
Schools

approach is better than what was done in the past. The importance of this stage of learning for a district cannot be overemphasized. The vast majority of districts should undertake improvement efforts even when they may be engaged with efforts at another level.

Stage 3 is a continuation of efforts initiated in the previous stage. Here the district is aware of changes in the broader society and begins to understand that the basic role and function of schools must be reexamined. The community's educational needs present the school with new opportunities, alternatives, and pressures. In this restructuring stage, schools frequently begin to envision a new role for themselves. They tend to look beyond the comparatively narrow view of schooling 5- to 18-year-olds to the much broader view of human resource development, which responds to the needs of the larger community. In this stage of evolution, the school may begin to serve new clients, develop new programs, extend outreach activities, adopt new management practices, extend financial capabilities and so on. Here the school is moving away from past structures, programs, and methods of delivery.

Stage 4 completes the evolutionary process as the school becomes a center or hub of a larger learning community. The school becomes a place where all can be served—a place where the range of intellectual, physical, and effective needs of people are recognized. The school serves cross-generational needs, and its programming reflects an understanding of the relationship among physical, emotional, and intellectual factors in the learning process. The school collaborates and is closely aligned with other learning opportunities found in businesses, social agencies, museums, and community groups. At this stage, the school has moved beyond the narrow definition of its role to a broader definition as a developer of human beings and a center for the exchange and processing of information.

Forces likely to move schools in this direction include:
- the increased demands for youth and adult learning and development programs,
- the realization of the need for support from larger segments of the community,
- the service delivery network provided by neighborhood schools,
- the value to staff and clients of a more integrated service program,
- the cost efficiency of using an existing physical and organizational network,
- the needs for multiple options for learning, and
- the competition that public schools will experience from private schools and other parts of the public sector.

## A New Role for Schools

Movement or evolution through the four stages outlined above will not be linear or consistent. Rather, small changes are likely as schools experiment and gain the skills and knowledge necessary to move into uncharted areas. The speed with which schools move into their new role will vary according to the capacities of their current systems and staffs, available leadership, community opportunities, and community pressures. Some districts may move quickly to add new services that are similar to their current functions, such as early childhood education and latch-key care programs. Others will develop partnerships with businesses to create new programs for high school students, recognizing their potential applications for adults. Still others will merge with organizations such as community colleges, museums, and job training institutions to strengthen community and organizational resources.

Educational improvement or restructuring does not happen as a result of national or state mandates. Change must be manifested at the local level and must be wanted—people must view change as their own and feel that it will help them achieve the future they value and desire. Strategic planning provides the process that helps give organizations a perspective of what is needed through a scanning of the external environment, a better understanding of their internal capacities, and a mission or common sense or direction for future growth and development.

# Chapter 2

# STRATEGIC PLANNING IN EDUCATION

The origin of strategic planning can be traced to the business community. General Electric has frequently been given credit for pioneering its use during the 1960s. Other corporations, however, also were beginning to realize that changes in the external environment were likely to have a greater impact on their survival than the internal matters over which they had control. With the emergence of the information society, increased competition from other countries, the rapid increase in oil prices, the environmental movement, and other changes, corporations began to see the need for anticipating change and responding to it to ensure their survival.

Today some form of strategic planning is practiced by most large corporations and an increasing number of smaller organizations. By the late 1970s, public agencies began to see its value and to adopt it to their own needs. A few farsighted school superintendents experimented with strategic planning with varying levels of success. An estimated 500 school districts currently engage in some form of strategic planning.

When a management technique is adapted to new settings, it passes through several stages of refinement and insight. During the initial stages of strategic planning by schools, emphasis was placed on the planning itself. For many it was seen as an extended form of long-range planning with the added steps of environmental scanning that was unlikely to have any great impact on the traditional role of the school. Other districts and schools have used parts of the strategic planning process, such as the analysis of internal organizational capacity to develop general improvement plans. These districts did not link their planning to respond to the needs of the larger community. However, some districts understand the potential of strategic planning to bring about organizational transformation. They have applied the technique not only to planning, but also to restructuring programs, management styles, clients, fiscal arrangements, and relationships with the community.

Experience with strategic planning suggests that it may have either minimal impact on a district or be a catalyst for district transformation. Its impact is determined by the beginning level of district/ school capacity, the leadership that backs the plan (energy and commitment of key people), the quality of the implementation plan, and the persistence in carrying out the plan.

# Definitions of Strategic Planning

Strategic planning is a rational process or series of steps that move an educational organization through:

1. understanding the external forces or changes relevant to it;
2. assessing its organizational capacity;
3. developing a vision (mission) of its preferred future as well as a strategic direction to follow to achieve that mission;
4. developing goals and plans that will move it from where it is to where it wants to be;
5. implementing the plans it has developed; and
6. reviewing progress, solving problems, and renewing plans.

Strategic planning obviously goes beyond a mechanistic series of planning procedures. Its power is in its capacity to create dissonance in people, upset old views, identify new possibilities, and pose new questions. In this sense, strategic planning is:

- a management process for changing and transforming organizations,
- a management philosophy,
- a way of thinking about and solving problems,
- an educational experience and staff development activity,
- an organizational development experience, and
- a community education and involvement process.

Transformation is the process of shifting our basic assumptions and reorganizing our views of the world, our goals, and our behaviors. Changes in society have occurred so rapidly and extensively as to warrant our calling this time an age of transition. At times such as this we must reexamine our assumptions about organizations, about programs, about management, and about our personal lives. We must also learn to adapt to the requirements of our changed environment. Strategic planning helps us carry out this process of reexamination and invention.

Strategic planning is a rational planning process, but it has strong psychological effects on an organization and the people involved in the process. Environmental scanning (external and internal) and the related educational processes raise powerful questions and issues for the organization and the individual. Some examples of questions raised by the process are provided below.

## Organizational Questions

1. How well are we preparing our children and youth for lives in a future society?
2. What is our community really like? How is it changing? What are the needs of the people in our community?
3. What do we assume/believe that we are doing? What are we really doing?
4. What do we see as our strengths, weaknesses, and future problems? How do these perceptions match the other information we've collected?
5. What information does our management system give us? What information do we need?
6. What are the threats to the strength or survival of our schools? What can we do to reduce these threats?
7. What roles might schools perform to meet community needs? What roles do we want them to perform?

## Individual Questions

1. What are the consequences of the changes in society for my professional and personal life?
2. What is the meaning of what I am doing? How does it fit with the larger scheme of things?
3. What are the possibilities for my involvement in valuable activities?
4. What does all of this mean for my long-range future? Will I be able to meet the new pressures and challenges?
5. Can I see shortcuts or new possibilities for accomplishing what I feel is important?
6. Where can I get help and support from others to protect myself and to change and grow?

Individual reactions to the environmental scanning and community/staff education process, which is an integral part of strategic planning, differ. For most people it is an opportunity to better understand and integrate insights they have already experienced; they welcome it and feel it adds some shape and direction to their current knowledge. Others, however, may regard the need for change as a threat because they are uncertain how they will fit into the changed conditions. Still others may choose to ignore the implications of the need for change.

Fortunately, the most common reaction is a high level of positive feelings and excitement. Those who become involved in the process reorient their assumptions about the world, the role of schools, and their own personal behaviors. They see new possibilities and a common direction for organizational growth and achievement. In some instances the excitement produced by the process and its possible effects on people's lives may make it so interesting that the planning and implementation work is forgotten. A case in point is a school district that became so interested in environmental scanning and futures activities that they set up an ongoing futures group for staff and a futures curriculum for students, but never got around to completing the stages of strategic planning.

Given the potential of strategic planning, it is difficult to find a definition that does justice to the purpose of strategic planning and its related impact on an organization. Definitions that have been put forward include:

> Strategic planning is a process of matching results of an assessment of an institution's external environment with the result of an institution's internal environment . . . [the process] should be to assist institutions to capitalize on strengths, minimize weaknesses, take advantage of opportunities, and eliminate or reduce threats.
>
> —Warren Goff

> Strategic planning is a vision of what the organization should be. It provides a framework which guides choices that determine the nature and direction of an organization.
>
> —Ben Tregoe

> Strategic planning is the process by which guiding members of an organization envision its future and develop the necessary procedures and operations to achieve that future.
>
> —Pfeiffer, Goodstein, and Nolan

The above definitions focus on the planning aspects and the framework strategic planning provides for decision making. Important as these may be, strategic planning, as used throughout this book, embraces a broader meaning:

> Strategic planning is a process for organizational renewal and transformation. This process provides a means of matching services and activities with changed and changing environmental conditions. Strategic planning provides a framework for the improvement and restructuring of programs, management, collaborations, and evaluation of the organization's progress.

Strategic planning is often thought of as a form of long-range planning. Although both types of planning are concerned with the future, there are structural differences between them. Long-range planning typically begins with an assumption that the organization will remain comparatively stable; it seeks to develop internal goals and projections based on that assumption. Strategic planning, on the other hand, begins with an examination of the external environment and using that information reexamines the basic role of the organization within the context of what is happening in the larger society. Other differences between strategic and long-range planning are provided in Figure 2-1.

Strategic planning within a district does not eliminate the need for traditional planning activities. Rather, it provides the framework

**Figure 2-1**
**Comparison of Strategic and Long-Range Planning**

| | Strategic Planning | Long-Range Planning |
|---|---|---|
| ASSUMES | an open system whereby organizations must constantly change as the needs of the larger society change. | a closed system within which short-range plans or blueprints are developed. |
| FOCUSES ON | the process of planning, building a vision, external environment, organizational capacity, staff and community education. | the final blueprint of a plan, internal analysis. |
| IS DONE BY | a small group of planners with widespread involvement of stakeholders. | a planning department or professionals. |
| USES | current and projected trends to make current decisions. | existing data on which to project future plans. |
| EMPHASIZES | changes outside the organization, organizational values, and proactive action. | internal changes, planning methods, inside-out planning. |
| FOCUS | asks what decision is appropriate *today* based on an understanding of the situation five years from now. | organizational goals and objectives five years from now. |
| DEPENDS UPON | intuitive and creative decision making as to how to guide the organization over time in an ever-changing environment; and an organizationwide process that anticipates the future, makes decisions, and behaves in light of an agreed-upon vision. | detailed and interrelated data sets, agency plans, and extrapolations of current budgets. |

*Adapted from Cope 1981*

or superordinate set (a mission and strategic goals) to guide other planning, decision making, and management.

In most school districts, planning should be implemented at three levels: in policy, in program development, and in program delivery. A primary use of strategic planning is at the policy level where the basic district mission, goals, and expectations for performance and outcomes are developed. Once formulated at the policy level, strategic planning provides a framework to guide program development and program delivery. A visual representation of these three levels of planning is provided in Figure 2-2.

Each planning level provides a different element for organizational success. Strategic planning addresses the *relevancy* of the total organizational program. It begins with the question, "What knowledge, skills, and capabilities will youth and adults need in the future?" Relevant programs meet the needs of the community and the clients served. Strategic planning requires the development of a vision or an approximation of the future that provides the assumptions for developing the organizational mission and strategic goals. The vision becomes the framework for program development and decision making.

Program planning addresses the issue of effectiveness. "Are we doing the things that will help us achieve our mission and goals?" This question may easily relate to curriculum and instructional systems, but it is equally important to review the budget, physical facilities, staff development, technology, personnel systems, and other factors to ensure that they support the attainment of the mission and goals.

| Figure 2-2 | | | |
|---|---|---|---|
| Levels of Planning in School Districts | | | |
| **Type of Planning** | **Responsibility** | **Outcome** | **Questions to Answer** |
| STRATEGIC PLANNING (Where are we going?) | Board and superintendent (with input from all groups) | Strategic plan, mission statement, goals, decision points | Are we going in the right direction? (relevance) |
| PROGRAM PLANNING (How do we get there?) | Central staff, principals (with input from teachers and staff) | Curriculum plan, personnel development plan, facilities plan, budget | Are we doing the right things to achieve our mission? (effectiveness) |
| PROGRAM DELIVERY PLANS (What do we do to get there?) | Teachers, counselors, staff (with input from parents, students, and the community) | Lesson plans, work plans | Are we doing things right? (efficiency) |

The third level of planning is for program delivery. Program delivery planning addresses the issue of efficiency. It asks, "How well are we doing things? Does the day-to-day delivery of services support the attainment of our mission and goals?"

It is important to note that high levels of achievement are possible only when each of these three planning elements is in place. A district's mission and goals may be relevant but not effective or efficient. A district may be effective, but its mission may not be relevant. The first stage of strategic planning may provide a mission and goals, but little will be achieved if it is not followed up with strong planning and implementation.

## The Phases of Strategic Planning

The decision to engage in strategic planning should not be made quickly or without serious consideration of the time and effort required to fully implement such a plan. Traditional planning often results in the preparation of an elegant document. The ultimate outcome of effective strategic planning, on the other hand, is organizationwide change or transformation.

Strategic planning in a public agency is a slower process than in the business world. Decision making in a school district, for example, is widely distributed. Although the board of education is the official governing body, administrators, unions, parents, and the business community may exert considerable influence on the district. If time is taken to involve affected and interested parties (stakeholders), the plan will become their plan, implementation will be accelerated, and the potential for future conflict and disagreement will be reduced.

A district should aim to have a written strategic plan together with a mission and strategic goals ready after one school year. Implementation plans should follow in about three months, and full implementation of the plan should be expected in 15 to 18 months. The first stage of plan development is usually characterized by a high level of excitement, tempered in later stages by a more realistic understanding of the effort required for implementation.

The initial values of strategic planning may be described as the development of community and staff awareness and consensus. A common data base derived from the external and internal scanning is a primary early outcome of strategic planning. Dialogue about the data collected transforms them to information that is widely shared among district stakeholders. Changes commonly observed during this period include a new vocabulary and dialogue. People begin to develop images of what might be.

Developing the strategic plan and, subsequently, the implementation plans, adds the element of realism to the planning process. While plans should never lose sight of a future vision, questions of how to actualize the vision require the difficult commitment to realize the vision. The district must focus on the question: "Will this action or activity lead us to our vision?"

The full organizational impact of strategic planning begins to be seen during implementation activities when people are involved in new or modified programs, activities, and behaviors. At later stages this process is widely integrated into district systems at all levels. One should realize that widespread organizational behavior will probably not be seen until a district has spent at least two to three years in this process, although there will be many positive outcomes before this time.

This time schedule can be accelerated if resources are available for additional staff, intensive training sessions, or if crisis situations dictate action. Decision makers, however, should realize that the scope of planning, implementing, and evaluation must be carried out while the district continues to function under the usual press of day-to-day operations.

Strategic planning may be organized into five general phases of effort or focus. Time and effort required for each phase is not equal, and activities may overlap, but the phases give a general sense of sequence and organization. These phases include:

Phase I: Creating a Base for Planning and Change
Phase II: Developing the Strategic Plan
Phase III: Developing the Implementation Plan
Phase IV: Implementing and Monitoring the Plan
Phase V: Renewing the Plan

(See fig. 2-3.) Activities and outcomes of each of these phases are discussed in the following sections.


## Phase I: Creating a Base for Planning and Change

Two primary sets of activities comprise the first phase of strategic planning: environmental scanning (i.e., gathering, analyzing, and preparing external and internal data) and community and staff education and involvement (i.e., stakeholder input). These activities, which create the base of information, common understanding, and support needed for subsequent planning, may be carried out concurrently during the first project phase. Each is discussed below.

## Figure 2-3
## Phases of Strategic Planning

| Phase I<br>Creating a Base for<br>Planning and Change | Phase II<br>Developing the<br>Strategic Plan | Phase III<br>Developing the<br>Implementation Plan | Phase IV<br>Implementating<br>and Monitoring<br>the Plan | Phase V<br>Renewing<br>the Plan |
|---|---|---|---|---|
| External Environmental Scanning and Analysis | Developmental Plan | Central Systems Plans | Reporting and Observing | Evaluating |
| Internal Organizational Scanning and Analysis | Review of Plan | Building Plans | Monitoring | |
| Stakeholder Input | Revision and Finalization of Plan | Correcting and Problem Solving | Replanning | |
| Community Education | | | | |

## Environmental Scanning

Environmental scanning is the generic term used to describe a series of activities aimed at providing an organization with the information it needs to make decisions about its present and future. The first three activities constitute external environmental scanning, and the last two constitute internal organizational analysis.

- *Trends analysis*—a series of economic, demographic, social, political, or educational developments that can be estimated or measured over time. Trend data are used to identify emerging trends and project future events.
- *Pattern analysis*—a detailed assessment of trend patterns and their possible and probable implications for schools.
- *Scenario decision points*—the projection of possible future events and how and when these are likely to affect schools.
- *Internal scanning*—a detailed analysis of the strengths, weaknesses, and capacity of the organization (e.g., district and schools).
- *Stakeholder perceptions and expectations*—information collected informally and systematically (e.g., through surveys, interviews, Delphi techniques, etc.) to identify community groups' perceptions and expectations of schools.

## External Environmental Scanning

The first goal of environmental scanning is to identify the nature of the community and changed and changing conditions likely to affect education and training systems. External environmental scanning begins with trends analysis in five general areas—economic, demographic, social, political, and educational. Some organizations also use the category of technology, but for public schools, technological trends can be included within each of the five areas outlined above. Trend information should be collected and analyzed at the national, state, regional (within state), and local levels.

Once identified, trends should be organized in terms of national, state, regional, and local patterns. These patterns should give an indication of whether the trend is increasing, decreasing, or staying about the same. The possible and probable implications for schools can then be extracted from these patterns to pinpoint possible pressures or effects on schools.

Last, the implications can be reviewed to develop short- or long-term scenarios or projections to predict how pressures or opportunities will manifest themselves and over what period of time. A visual representation of this process is provided in Figure 2-4.

*Trends Analysis.* Completing a trends analysis of each of these five areas could be overwhelming. The goal is to develop a comprehensive yet concise picture of the trends most likely to affect schools.

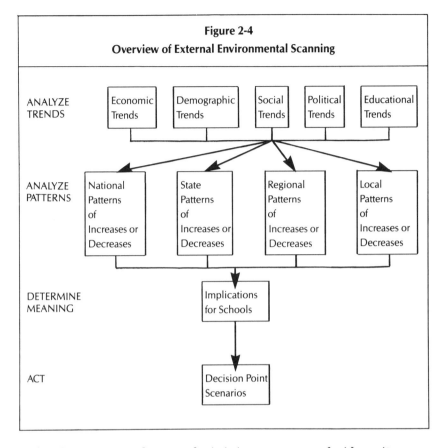

**Figure 2-4**
**Overview of External Environmental Scanning**

ANALYZE TRENDS: Economic Trends | Demographic Trends | Social Trends | Political Trends | Educational Trends

ANALYZE PATTERNS: National Patterns of Increases or Decreases | State Patterns of Increases or Decreases | Regional Patterns of Increases or Decreases | Local Patterns of Increases or Decreases

DETERMINE MEANING: Implications for Schools

ACT: Decision Point Scenarios

Before beginning such an analysis it is necessary to decide on its scope and the time and effort you can devote to it. Examples of the types of information that might be covered are outlined in Appendix B, "External Scanning Data Checklist."

It is important to note that many organizations have already undertaken strategic planning. Consequently, there now exists an abundance of material already collected and available to those about to start their own strategic planning. Resources for environmental scanning materials are local Chambers of Commerce and United Way agencies; state, regional, and local planning agencies; corporations; and businesses. Many of these organizations have information about strategic planning on the national, state, or local level. Newspapers, magazine articles, and studies carried out by universities or government agencies are also important sources of data.

When reviewing information for use in trends analysis, ensure that the data are recent (within the past five years) and that the most relevant data are selected for review. In most instances more information will be identified than can profitably be used. Persons preparing the materials must continually "boil the trends down" to extract the information most relevant to schools.

*Pattern Analysis.* After the trend data have been collected, a second type of reduction process is probably needed to uncover patterns and relationships. Pattern analysis can be a fairly simple collection of projected trends or directions. Examples of pattern analysis are found in Appendix C, with an example of the next step, identifying scenario decision points. It is important to pay particular attention to this aspect of the scanning process. Many districts analyze the changes in their environment but fail to consider the consequences for their schools. They simply move ahead, developing internal improvement plans using the evidence of a changed environment as general background rather than seeing it as a threat or as an opportunity to change their organizations.

*Scenario Decision Points.* The last step in external environmental scanning is developing projections or scenarios of what is likely to happen. A critical and ongoing task throughout strategic planning and strategic management is building images or visions of the future. Building these images or visions is a process of successive approximation. Our visions will continually become more refined as we gather and analyze information about trends.

Throughout this imaging of the future, we need to consider what is likely to happen or what could happen if a decision were made to intervene and act. These scenarios help us clarify the consequences of the decisions we might make. For example, with respect to the overall role of public education, we can imagine four basic scenarios (see fig. 2-5).

| | |
|---|---|
| Scenario A: | Traditional values remain, and reform succeeds in reaffirming and gaining support for public schools. |
| Scenario B: | Transformed values develop, and schools succeed in moving into new areas of service and support. |
| Scenario C: | Traditional values remain and reform fails; schools remain under fire with diminished support, increased competition, and a loss of power in the community. |
| Scenario D: | Transformed values remain, but reform fails; schools are part of segmented communities. |

These four scenarios make basic assumptions about two major sets of variables—the nature and success or failure of reform efforts, and the societal values likely to prevail. In the first instance, reform may

**Figure 2-5**
**Scenarios for Public Education**

| | Individual Segmented Values | Collaborative Integrative Values |
|---|---|---|
| Educational Reform | Improvement | Restructuring |
| WORKS | Scenario A<br><br>Public schools affirmed for traditional role | Scenario B<br><br>Learning communities with expanded role and support for schools |
| FAILS | Scenario C<br><br>Schools under fire; diminished support and competition | Scenario D<br><br>Segmented schools and communities |

Adapted from "Scenarios: A Tool For Planning in Uncertain Times," the United Way.

remain within the values of an industrial society: individualistic, competitive, and narrowly defined outcomes. Or reform may move to new levels of restructuring in a society with more collaborative, integrative values. In either case the efforts devoted to reform may succeed or fail.

The above example is a relatively broad scenario that could help develop a mission. Other more limited scenarios or story lines could be useful in helping a group understand the meaning of trends and their implications.

The outcome of external environmental scanning should be the discovery of what is in the environment, what this means for schools, and some general ideas or story lines of how things will evolve and change.

## Internal Organizational Analysis

The focus of the second form of scanning—the internal organizational analysis—is on where the organization is and what it can do. This organizational analysis provides information for strategic planning and supplies important information for the overall improvement of the organization.

Internal organizational analysis may be carried out in a variety of ways, but the goal is to gain an overall picture of how well the organization is performing. It is an in-depth view of strengths, weaknesses, gaps, and issues facing the district.

The actual process of internal scanning may be organized in a fashion similar to external scanning. A model for internal organizational analysis developed by the Detroit Public Schools outlines the way that internal school issues may be viewed in economic, social, political, educational, and technological terms—a structure that parallels external scanning. Technology was added as a separate category given the effort to utilize technology in schools. A visual representation of this structure is provided in Figure 2-6.

An internal organizational analysis begins with an in-depth review of the five areas for scanning. Some types of data that would be collected and reviewed in each area are included in Appendix D, "Internal Scanning Data Checklist." These areas should be adapted to fit the specific needs of the school district. In each area, an effort should be made to use past patterns and future projections to develop trends. Microcomputer graphics can aid in understanding by displaying trend lines over time, providing a visual way to identify possible issues.

A summary and the effective presentation of data are important to the plan's success. People must be able to understand the data and grasp the issues.

Preparation of an overall assessment (executive summary) is a helpful step. It should provide the reader with a balanced overview of the current state of the organization and its future capacity for devel-

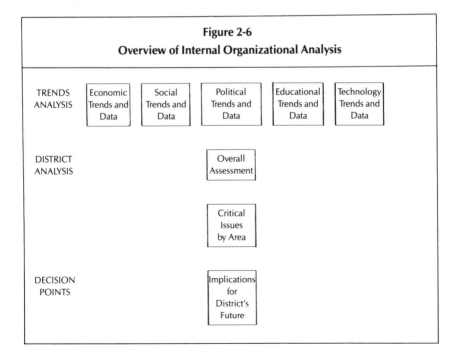

**Figure 2-6**
**Overview of Internal Organizational Analysis**

| TRENDS ANALYSIS | Economic Trends and Data | Social Trends and Data | Political Trends and Data | Educational Trends and Data | Technology Trends and Data |
| --- | --- | --- | --- | --- | --- |

DISTRICT ANALYSIS — Overall Assessment

Critical Issues by Area

DECISION POINTS — Implications for District's Future

opment. The assessment may be followed by a listing of the issues in each area and potential implications for the district. Implications should frame the areas where decisions are required for future plans.

Internal organizational analysis usually requires a considerable amount of effort if the district has not established information systems. A common outcome for districts is the establishment of district and/or building management information systems (MIS) using the data from the internal organizational analysis. Such a system greatly facilitates not only the monitoring of the plan but also the improvement of district and building management.

*Stakeholder Perceptions and Expectations.* A characteristic of public institutions is the large number of people and groups who have an interest or stake in their success (stakeholders). Decisions about the future of a public organization (e.g., a school system) should display an understanding of and take into account the perceptions and expectations of the various stakeholder groups. Information about their perceptions and expectations must be gathered carefully. It should be collected after stakeholders have had some opportunity to understand the larger societal changes and the options open to schools.

This can be accomplished in a number of ways. Staff, board, community groups, business groups, and others may be invited to participate in seminars, task forces, conferences, study sessions, or other forms of education or involvement prior to collecting data. It is often better to present information on societal changes over a period of time to allow for proper understanding.

When time is not available, data collection should still be preceded by information presented either orally or in writing. Stakeholders should comment on their perceptions of organizational strengths and weaknessses and their visions of how schools might develop in the future. At this stage it is usually wise to avoid overly specific questions. What is needed is information about stakeholders' perceptions of the school's future role and activities.

*Community Education.* One purpose of strategic planning is to help people understand change in the larger society and anticipate the effects of this change on the school, on their jobs, and on students. Equipped with this awareness, people frequently revise their assumptions about the world and develop new educational practice and leadership skills.

Those involved in this process are likely to develop greater knowledge and skills in:

- developing new sources of data and scanning in their personal environment and experience to develop and test new ideas,
- increasing their awareness of goals and how their activities contribute to goal attainment,

- looking for and developing alternatives for problem solving,
- anticipating problems by thinking through or imagining possible next steps, and
- understanding their relatedness to others and looking for opportunities to collaborate.

The degree to which such skills develop depends on the opportunities to review information and think through the implications for the current and desired organizational climate. This education process should also include information on strategic planning and an explanation of why the district is moving ahead with a strategic planning effort.

Many groups, especially staff members, need time to understand changes in the larger society and how they relate to schools. They also need to be reassured that any changes in the school system will not be arbitrary and that they will be given adequate time to prepare to learn any necessary new skills.

It is only natural that some degree of resistance may develop at this or later points. Change that is not understood or desired may be threatening; trading the current status quo for an uncertain future may seem unwise. Strategic planning directly addresses these feelings by providing better information and giving people a sense of control over their futures rather than a feeling that they can only react to changes as they occur.

Educating the community about strategic planning should be carefully planned. Seminars, workshops, or other sessions may be scheduled to provide in-depth information to the community. Presentations at meetings of service clubs, social welfare groups, parent groups, and professional associations will extend general understanding. Staff in-service, informal staff meetings, task forces, and other methods can be used to involve and inform the staff. Futures courses for secondary students will increase student understanding as well as involve the faculty.

Scheduling these types of community education and involvement activities prior to collecting data generally increases the quality of the information gathered. But it is important to note that community education and involvement must continue throughout the strategic planning process. Stakeholders need periodic progress reports as well as an opportunity to air their ideas and reactions.

### Summary

This first phase of strategic planning is extremely important. The quality of information collected and the way it is organized will determine the scope of understanding during actual plan development. Involving community groups and staff effectively creates an open climate, establishes the trust necessary for plan development and implementation, and ensures a common base of information upon which understanding can develop.

This phase of planning will probably take one school year unless the district has already been engaged in preparatory activities. It is essential that top management (the superintendent) endorses the process and supports staff work. It also is important that adequate staff resources be allocated to the task and that the staff has direct access to the superintendent.

While a great deal of effort goes into this phase of planning, many of the activities have meaning and significance for the district beyond the development of the plan. The collection of internal data sets the stage for ongoing management information systems. The collection of external data provides a baseline for decision making, and the community education effort creates a common framework of understanding for decision making and improved interorganizational relationships.

## Phase II: Developing the Strategic Plan

Who should be involved in the planning? Selection of the individuals to develop the plan may be done in a variety of ways. Because the strategic plan is a framework for district policy, the policymakers (board members) must be involved in some meaningful way.

The board and top management may be the primary work group to review the environmental analyses, identify and review implications, and develop scenarios or formulate a vision for the school district. A group of top management staff may develop alternatives and then involve board members in a second review and preliminary formulation of a plan. Another approach is to appoint a task force of knowledgeable community and staff members to review the data and prepare the initial formulation of the plan.

The local situation and trust level among groups should be considered when determining the best method to use. Bringing in knowledgeable business people is a means of ensuring a broader range of experience and perspective. It may be useful to bring in the top staff and teacher representatives at an early stage of the process. The formulation of the planning group will shape expectations about the plan and its implementation. Regardless of the method used, continuing communication with and the provision for input from all groups are essential.

The planning group should be kept small enough for meaningful discussion (probably not more than 12 to 18 persons), but larger groups can be used with a skillful combination of small- and large-group discussion and work. It may be wise to have one or two outside facilitators to keep things moving smoothly and to provide information and content. Facilitators are especially useful in helping the planning group deal with external and internal scanning data. Since they are not part of the school system, they are frequently able to handle sensitive issues, make sure everyone gets a chance to speak, and clarify different points of view.

The first consideration of the environmental scanning data should allow for an intensive period during which people can devote their full attention to the task. A retreat of two to three days away from the organizational setting is usually advisable. Facilitators should ensure that adequate time is available for an in-depth analysis of the scanning data before launching into a discussion of the strategic plan itself. It may even be advisable to schedule work sessions—a two- to three-day session to review the scanning data and a second retreat or work session to develop the plan after people have had time to consider the scanning data.

**Ideas to Consider**

How does a group arrive at a strategic plan, and what should such a plan look like? Thought processes do not follow a linear path. Nonetheless, a general sequence of ideas to consider in developing a strategic plan is presented below.

*Review of External Scanning:*
- Where is the community?
- What are the national, state, regional, and local trends?
- What implications are they likely to have for schools in our community?
- What opportunities (needs) are there in the community?
- What threatens the future well-being of schools in our community?
- What activities might be developed in the future?

*Review of Internal Scanning:*
- Where is our organization?
- What are our organizational strengths? (staff, curriculum, food service, business management, staff development, etc.)
- What are the critical issues facing our organization?
- What internal steps (improvement) must be taken to strengthen our organization?
- Where are the possible "matches" between community opportunities (needs) and the resources and strengths of our organization?

*Developing a Vision:*
- What is our preferred future?

- What would we like to see our organization doing five years from now?
- What role would we like to have schools perform in the future?
- What should be the core purpose or mission of our schools?
- What things do we value most about our schools and the ways they operate?
- What words or phrases describe our belief (philosophy) and the mission we want for our schools?

*Developing Strategic Goals:*

- How might we achieve our preferred future?
- What general or large tasks do we need to accomplish if we are to achieve our preferred future? (These should require some time to accomplish.)
- Over what time period should these tasks be accomplished?
- What will we have accomplished in five years?

The outcome of this activity should be a first draft of the strategic plan. The plan itself should be a concise document—one that sets guidelines for the development of schools in the community. Items commonly included in strategic plans are:

- the need for a strategic plan,
- philosophic beliefs and planning assumptions,
- district mission, and
- district strategic goals.

The initial plan should be reviewed by stakeholder groups. The planning group need not respond to every suggestion but should carefully consider comments and suggestions for revision. This process will improve the quality of the proposed plan, provide valuable information about future issues, and encourage a feeling of stakeholder ownership of the plan.

After reviewing suggestions and comments of stakeholders, a final version of the strategic plan should be drafted and adopted by the school board. It should be understood that the plan is not only a guide for staff and program implementation but also a framework for policy and decision making.

## Summary

The final version of the district strategic plan should be a comparatively straightforward, concise document outlining the preferred future of the district. A good strategic plan should include:

- a statement that addresses community and school needs and assumptions about the future;
- a mission, stated as an ideal purpose or vision around which people can organize their energies and efforts (an image of what people desire for the future);

- strategic goals for the larger organization, tasks necessary to attain the vision, general long-range goals (for three to five years); and
  - a plan that is clearly written and easily understood by readers.

The final document may not encompass every identified expectation or desire. This is normal. It should, however, provide a sense of direction and identify the primary goals to pursue to move in the desired direction. Most districts need about three months to develop the plan, but the process should not be delayed for long. It is better to move on, making modifications after the plan has been implemented.

## Phase III: Developing the Implementation Plan

The strategic plan sets forth the mission and goals of the district. It provides a general map, not a blueprint or overly specific directions. It should be viewed as a statement of where the district is going.

The implementation plan, on the other hand, employs traditional planning methods to reach the stated destination. Strategic planning has often been likened to navigating a convoy of ships: the strategic plan establishes the destination, such as London, and the convoy's mission, which is to get there safely. But the way each ship gets there varies. Individual ships may alter their courses to avoid storms, make repairs, refuel, and so on, but they all have a common destination.

So, too, the strategic plan states the destination, but the implementation plan fills in the ways in which this destination is to be reached. Implementation plans are usually developed for a year but may be extended for a longer time period. Implementation plans should be developed for districtwide systems (physical facilities, personnel, community relations, curriculum, instruction, staff development, technology, etc.) and for individual schools. In each instance it is important to remember that implementation plans are likely to cover many areas not included in the strategic plan. It is necessary that they be aligned with the strategic plan so they do not retard progress toward accomplishing the strategic goals.

Implementation plans should be developed by those responsible for carrying them out. This requires that principals and central office staff have an in-depth understanding of the plans they are to implement. The plans, however, must be coordinated by some central planning group. It is essential to maintain a balance and creative tension between district and building goals and among district system plans. A districtwide mission or strategic vision makes it possible to see functional connections between these levels. Top management and the school board then must ensure that implementation plans are consistent with the strategic plan.

Developing implementation plans is not to be taken lightly. It requires time to involve key staff and for them, in turn, to involve their staff. For example, principals should be encouraged to involve teachers in building plans. Central staff will want to include key people in developing their plans. In an ideal situation, staff would meet two or three weeks before school opens. They would then have time for intensive planning. There would be time for general sessions to outline the planning purposes and procedures, report general progress, and coordinate plans. There would also be time for small-group sessions to develop plans, and free time to create daily work plans. Where this is not possible, planning may extend over a longer period of time. Even in this case, however, it is best to block out shorter time periods for intensive planning.

Implementation plans should be as specific as possible. A format often used for planning at this level is provided in Figure 2-7. Other formats for implementation plans may also be appropriate. If district personnel are familiar with a specific type of planning methodology, so much the better. Using it will probably speed up development. A good implementation plan outline includes goals, objectives, specific activities, timelines, responsibilities, and outcomes. Where district staff have significant planning experience, it may be useful to develop specific indicators for evaluation. This is particularly appropriate when district staff includes planning personnel.

### Summary

The strategic plan addresses the question of relevancy or a long-range look at where the district is going. The implementation plan addresses the question of effectiveness. It offers a short-range look at how the district intends to achieve the mission and goals outlined in the strategic plan. Ultimate success of any strategic plan will be determined by the quality of the implementation plan. The implementation plan guides the staff while providing a yardstick for evaluating the progress of the district, the central office, and the building. It provides a basic management tool and framework for staff and program evaluation.

## Phase IV: Implementing and Monitoring the Plan

Upon completion of the implementation plan, emphasis shifts to strategic management (i.e., the incorporation of the strategic plan into the day-to-day activities of the district). During this phase, administrators and supervisors are responsible for implementation. This shift cannot occur unless efforts are made to prepare the staff and provide it with the knowledge and skills necessary for implementation.

**Figure 2-7**

**Example of an Implementation Goal**

**Goal:** To improve instruction in Minto Valley School.

**Objective:** To increase the number of instructional methodologies used by teachers in every classroom and to increase student achievement by 5 percent on tests.

| Activity | Timeline | Responsibility | Outcome |
|---|---|---|---|
| 1.1 Review range of instructional methods and systems | September | Principal, committee of teachers, staff development resource persons | Identification of instructional models and systems |
| 1.2 Facilitate session with teachers to review instructional systems and models | October | Staff developer | Knowledge of instructional models and systems |
| 1.3 Select priority models to be implemented | October | Teachers/principal | Years priority for instructional model |
| 1.4 Schedule and implement training sessions | November and December | Staff developer/principal | Trained staff |
| 1.5 Organize peer teams to coach teachers | | Principal | Support/observational teams |
| 1.6 Arrange time for observation | | Principal | Plan for observation |
| 1.7 Collect observation data during selected times | February | Principal/teachers | Data about use of model or system |
| 1.8 Review data with teachers | March | Staff developer | Informed staff |
| 1.9 Conduct second observational sample | April | Principal | Data about efficiency of model implementation |
| 1.10 Report findings to staff | May | Staff developer/principal | Informed staff |
| 1.11 Involve staff in discussion model—identification of problems | May | Staff developer | Staff input of evaluation of project |
| 1.12 Evaluate use of instructional model | June | Teachers/principal | Report on implementation of the model |

## Implementation

Staff development is critical at this stage. It furthers the goals of the strategic plan and is a necessary element for building understanding and shaping district culture. This in turn promotes the plan. Staff development should provide a mix of three activities. One should be generic sessions that provide common information and skills to all staff. A second form of staff development should be role- or building-specific, addressing the needs of a group of staff. A third form of staff development should include developmental activities such as providing expert information as part of curriculum development, sessions on educational research, and exploratory activities wherein individuals attend conferences, seminars, or other activities to update their general knowledge.

## Monitoring

It is also essential to check the progress of the district and building plans. This can be done using simple reports and computerized systems. Monitoring should be directed at early problem identification, and this information should be open to all personnel. Regular reports to staff, board, and community members will help maintain enthusiasm and continuity.

Goals are more easily reached when people can see progress. This can be done by regular personnel evaluation or in more public ways (celebrations, progress reports, etc.). Small task forces or committees may be formed to monitor various plans and provide reports to appropriate groups.

## Summary

If the strategic plan requires planning and support, so does the implementation plan. Throughout the implementation process, two systems are especially important: staff development and personnel and program evaluation. Even in a decentralized or school-based management structure, some degree of centralized or generic staff development is essential to build common understanding. This need not conflict with building needs that address specific program efforts or products. In most instances, however, inservice should be provided for personnel with like responsibilities, thereby ensuring acquisition of a common understanding and skills required for implementation. This is especially true if the strategic plan includes new types of program efforts and behaviors.

Monitoring the implementation of a plan is essential for identifying problems at an early stage, documenting progress, and developing a framework for evaluation. Monitoring sets the stage for the final phase of renewal.

## Phase V: Renewing the Plan

Strategic plans are designed to provide a sense of direction for a relatively long period. In most instances the strategic plan will remain relevant over time. It should be recognized, however, that situations change, and we will learn and gain experience from implementing plans. It is important to set aside time to carefully evaluate the plan and to renew and modify it to reflect new insights and learnings.

Evaluation and renewal of the strategic plan should be undertaken annually at least. Questions to consider during this process include:

- What conditions have changed in the external environment since we wrote the strategic plan?
- What conditions have changed within our organization since we wrote the plan?
- Do the assumptions we made still apply?
- Do the mission statement and strategic goals continue to express our vision of schools and the things we need to do to reach that vision?
- Have we learned anything from our implementation efforts that would require modifications in our strategic plan?

These questions can help us decide if any modifications of the strategic plan are in order. Only when this has been done should the implementation plan be revised.

### Summary

Evaluation and renewal of the strategic plan prove the dynamic nature of strategic planning. The written plan communicates direction and understanding, but the most important feature of strategic planning is its value as a process. Strategic planning requires us to continually scan environments, become aware of changes and opportunities, develop a sense of direction and purpose, and organize our energies within that purpose to plan tasks and activities to reach our goals. As a result, we learn from our experience and improve. Living with strategic planning is learning to live with change. It is learning to maintain stability and balance in a world of change, and it is learning that people can work together to create their future.

# Chapter 3

# STRATEGIC MANAGEMENT AND LEADERSHIP

## An Organizational Development Tool

"Planning" is likely to conjure up images of written plans, which outline mission, goals, objectives, schedules, and responsibilities. Often these written plans remain on the shelf, important only to document accountability rather than to put forth dynamic concepts.

Strategic planning provides an opportunity to move beyond paper plans—to use the process to strengthen, and in some instances to transform, the organization. The ultimate outcome of strategic planning is strategic management, whereby individuals learn to incorporate the planning process into their daily behavior.

The power of the strategic planning process lies in its compatibility with new forms of management. Organizational changes are a natural outcome of the larger transformation of our society from an industrial to an information one. Organizational changes, in turn, call for major shifts in our managerial assumptions and practices. We realize that past responses to management have not always been effective and that we must now look for better ways of managing districts.

Strategic planning speaks to four major elements that can significantly improve the management systems of most districts. These are:

1. the development of information systems for decision making,
2. a common sense of direction,
3. stakeholder participation, and
4. linkages among units.

# Development of Information Systems for Decision Making

School districts regularly collect a variety of data about students, staff, expenditures, achievement, and so on. The data are sent to the state agency or filed without being analyzed or converted into information that might be used for decision making.

School personnel frequently do not have ready access to such data, which may be stored at a central office, making it inconvenient for staff members to read or analyze them. Even when board members have the data at hand, they may not take the time to discuss their implications to reveal the larger picture of the school system.

Lacking systematic knowledge of such data may mean that school personnel are not fully aware of enrollment projection studies or fiscal problems. Similarly, school personnel may have little insight into changes in the characteristics of the district's student population.

A primary principle underlying strategic planning is that data are collected and analyzed *before* any decisions about the organization's mission and goals are made. For most districts this data collection (environmental scanning—external and internal) is most useful. It demonstrates the value and the use of information in decision making. Most important, it provides a common data base for all stakeholders— board members, administrators, teachers, parents, community members, and students. Such an open system is essential for creating understanding among all the groups involved in district planning.

A district data base often provides a baseline of information for decision making. Many districts come to see the value of environmental scanning and allocate the necessary resources to maintain an updated information system. Some districts move the management information system (MIS) to the building level. A microcomputer in the principal's office can be used to develop a building MIS that provides the principal and teachers with ready access to student records, budgetary records or documents, attendance records, and so on. This places the vital information closer to the decision-making site and supports the staff in day-to-day decision making.

# A Common Sense of Direction

Relations between employers and employees in the United States are based, in large measure, on a mutual convenience: an organization needs an employee, the employee needs a job. Organizations are more commonly enclaves of people with independent needs rather than close-knit teams working for a common goal.

The autonomy of teachers has long been recognized as a positive value, part of the professional nature of teaching itself. But this autonomy traditionally has not been valued, and many school districts have attempted to organize themselves into strict hierarchies—top-down bureaucracies. Principals, caught in the middle, found themselves carrying out district mandates.

Top-down, autocratic management may work well on the assembly line, but management theory now recognizes that information workers require a different form of management. They typically require substantial autonomy if they are to perform their tasks at a high skill level. In this context, the role of the manager is to support workers and to coordinate their efforts toward achieving a mission and common goal. Teachers, one of the original categories of information workers, have resented top-down, rigid forms of supervision, primarily due to the lack of clarity about the overall direction of their activities. Today's management procedures recognize that building commitment to common goals unites staff and gives meaning to daily activities.

The autonomy of the teacher or the building principal does not detract from the importance of central systems. Districts still have the primary responsibility of developing the district mission, goals, and systems that will tie together the efforts of buildings and employees. Districts or other organizations that fail to provide a common sense of direction may be called *segmental organizations*.[51] Segmental organizations compartmentalize events, actions, and problems; each sphere remains isolated. Segmental organizations tend to resist change; individual or separate units cannot see the advantage of change for the total organization. Organizations more successful at change are termed *integrated organizations*. Separate units maintain a sense of totality and view their roles as part of the larger whole.

Strategic planning focuses on the development of a mission, a common sense of direction, or district goals. This umbrella of purpose provides a tight-loose type of management.[52] The mission and district goals are the "tight" portion of the system. They provide the common direction, expectations of outcomes, and standards of performance. This is *what* is to be accomplished. The "loose" part of the system is *how* these tasks are to be accomplished. "How" decisions must be made at the building level. Principals and teachers must have the opportunity to use building resources to meet the unique needs of students.

Strategic planning requires the development of a mission and goals to serve as the framework for building and central office implementation plans. It is not uncommon for this process to arouse resistance from staff, especially among those at middle-management level. Development of such plans inevitably requires integration among the various levels of the system. In most instances this necessitates a shift in the balance of power of the various groups. It also calls for greater collaboration among the staff. In many instances the organization moves from independent units to a greater sense of interdependency.

The mission and goals provide not only a common direction for the district but also represent an affirmation of common values. The language of a district mission may appear rather commonplace, but for groups who have worked through the process of agreeing on a mission, it frequently assumes a higher level of meaning and becomes a source of energy for those involved.

An organization's mission projects an image of what the organization is going to do; it may include how and where it will be done. The mission should have a sense of direction, suggest activities or programs, and provide motivation. For example, a district mission organized around "building a learning community" is likely to have a different vision than a district mission organized around "achieving the highest levels of excellence possible for all students." While each mission might be appropriate for a specific organization, the articulation of the vision and its implied values becomes a cohesive force for the organization.

Management in organizations such as school districts must rely primarily on persuasion and leadership rather than authority. The sharing of a goal or common sense of direction becomes an essential component of effective management and an essential element of "keeping the herd moving roughly West."

## Stakeholder Participation

Public agencies are inherently more difficult to manage than private institutions in that decision making is widely distributed and influenced by a significant number of groups. Although the school board is the official governing body for the district, parents, unions, business groups, students, and special interest groups can exert considerable influence on decision making. These groups cannot be ignored if schools wish to retain a high level of community support.

Given the importance and scope of strategic planning, the various interest groups or stakeholders must be brought into the process. A first step in strategic planning, therefore, is to involve these groups in educational activities related to environmental scanning. This provides stakeholder groups with a common understanding of changes taking place in society, in the community, and within the schools. Building this base of common understanding may be accomplished in a variety of ways—through seminars, readings, newspaper articles, videotapes, films, television, and so on.

Providing people with data *before* asking for their opinions and ideas about what schools should do leads to different responses and outcomes. Possession of such information frequently requires individuals to reexamine their assumptions. The awareness of dissonance between past or present assumptions and reality provides the energy for transformation and action.

Participation of various groups is not limited to the initial phase of strategic planning. If the process is to have meaning it must be maintained throughout the planning and implementation stages. Participation gives rise to expectations of continuing involvement. If there is no follow through (i.e., if participation is curtailed), conflict or lowered morale may occur.

Participation must be managed carefully. It must be meaningful to be effective. Managers must be sensitive to those decisions that are important to employees as opposed to decisions that are routine or technical. The history and culture of every district and school will determine the areas in which participation is important. A seemingly unimportant decision about something as small as the method of distributing books may be important because of the way this situation was handled in the past. Strategic planning can set the stage for new, positive levels of participative management.

## Linkage Among Units

In large organizations it is extremely difficult to build coordination among units and develop a strong sense of teamwork. A first step toward accomplishing this is to develop a district mission or vision of where the organization is headed. This vision must be operational and concrete. Implementation plans determine how a district is going to realize its vision. Directions outlined in these plans provide opportunities for top management to check on how well the mission and goals are understood and accepted.

Effective school districts are those in which the core technical systems support the districts' primary responsibility to provide quality curriculum and instruction—the basis for academic excellence.[53] The mission provides the criteria for judging the adequacy of implementation plans and a way to determine whether these plans agree with or will contribute to the attainment of the mission and goals.

Implementation plans may be organized in a variety of ways. Districts decide on the best ways to develop these plans. A district may decide to begin slowly, focusing implementation plans in a few areas, or it may decide to work in many areas if this accords with its strategic plan. An overview of possible implementation plans is found in Figure

3-1, which highlights the superordinate nature of the mission and the strategic plan. There are two primary sets of systems—structural sys-

**Figure 3-1**

DISTRICT VALUES AND PHILOSOPHY

POLICIES, MISSION, AND STRATEGIC PLAN

**Support Structural Systems**

- Organizational Structure
- Administrative System and Procedures
- Physical Facilities
- Budgeting and Accounting
- Personnel System
- Staff Evaluation
- Auxiliary Services
- Union Relations
- Community Outreach

**Program Delivery Systems**

- Needs Assessment and Data Base
- District Goals and Objectives
- Building Goals and Objectives
- District Plans
- Building Plans
- Curriculum "What"
- Instruction "How"
- Program Evaluation and Student Evaluation
- Staff Development
- Rewards and Reinforcement
- Parent Involvement

tems and program systems. Although the importance of each system is not equal, it illustrates the number of variables that can influence the success of the mission and district goals. Activities carried out in both systems must advance the district plan. This coordination of plans not only clarifies content and goals but facilitates team relationships by articulating expectations and standards.

Linkage issues will not be totally solved by coordinating implementation plans. One of the most difficult areas is likely to be the tension between district and building goals. District goals should not cover every aspect of schools' activities. Rather, they should sketch out the general direction and common expectations in some areas, recognizing that each building will need to develop its own goals as well.

## Four Steps Toward Organizational Excellence

In summary, strategic planning naturally lends itself to organizational development activities. Four areas of strategic planning that move naturally to strategic management and organizational development are outlined in Figure 3-2.

A shared data base, a vision (mission or sense of direction), participation, and linkage are necessary preconditions for organizational excellence. Their existence in a district makes possible organizational transformation. Simply shuffling individuals or developing a set of

| Figure 3-2 | | |
|---|---|---|
| **Area** | **Strategic Planning Activities** | **Strategic Management Activities** |
| SHARED DATA BASE | • Environmental scanning<br>— External<br>—Internal | • Management information systems<br>• Ongoing scanning activities<br>• Community/staff education |
| COMMON DIRECTION | • Mission and strategic goals<br>• Community education | • Reinforcement of mission<br>• Sense of ownership |
| PARTICIPATION | • Development of implementation plans | • Improved morale<br>• Interpersonal trust |
| LINKAGE | • Implementation plans | • Coordination and alignment |

plans will not produce the organizational change needed. The structures and systems of the district must be put in place to attain the desired program activities. While strategic planning frequently exposes the need for organizational development, it can also point to the steps required to align and improve district systems.

A word about timelines is useful. Strategic planning is a process, not an event. The planning process usually leads to efforts to achieve strategic management. This takes time. To achieve the full benefits of the process, the board and top management should be committed for four to five years. Naturally, the progress and outcomes of such an effort will be influenced by the resources devoted to the process.

Achieving strategic management in school systems entails changing the behavior of managers and decision makers. Not only must the structure of strategic planning and strategic management be put into place, but effort must also be devoted to providing support and training to the staff members who implement the plans. This empowerment of staff in helping them to learn new skills is an essential component of strategic management.

## Leadership: Requirement and Opportunity

A serious look at strategic planning reveals that it is not a casual endeavor. Strategic planning combines what we know is necessary for change with our changed understanding of what constitutes exemplary management practice. It is a tool that must be used to develop a vision to meet the needs of schools and the larger society.

The United States is still in a transitional era. The information society gives us hope for a new and improved way of life. To achieve this we must build a new culture—a culture of shared understanding and commitment to the common good. Education and training must be aimed at demonstrating how to achieve this culture. Schools must lead the way. They must meet the human needs of their local communities and give to one and all, youth and adults, the tools to prosper in our changing society.

Equal opportunity is a fundamental issue for schools. How equal can opportunity be? Youth, in increasing numbers, depend largely on public resources. The inequality of our current situation is evident when elementary school test scores can predict with remarkable accuracy whether a child will share her future with the "haves" or the "have nots" of society. If youth are to be prepared for full participation in an increasingly diverse and complex world, what is the role of the school?

Schools have a powerful influence on the lives of children. They can perform increasingly powerful services for all community groups. But schools must expand their development of human resources. There was a time, perhaps, when people did not need to function intellectually, physically, or emotionally at today's high levels, but that day is past. Our nation cannot tolerate the waste of human potential, nor can we stand by and allow race, income, sex, and other factors to determine the course of a child's destiny.

Children belong to everyone. Society must make a commitment and assume the responsibility for preparing children for the future. Our survival as a nation is at stake. The technological and individual accomplishments of Americans are impressive, but we have a long way to go to meet the needs of all our people. We must remember that we share a common fate.

To move schools in line with community needs and instill new meaning and goals, we must find people with commitment to common goals. Strategic planning offers the means to make this happen, but it cannot happen in a vacuum. It requires leadership at the local level: classroom teachers, principals, central staff members, superintendents, board members, parents, business persons, and interested citizens. These leaders need help to understand not only the technical aspects of improving and restructuring schools, but how these activities fit into a larger pattern of changing community cultures.

"Transformation" is a term used throughout this book in reference to the need for changing assumptions and developing common goals and directions. Strategic planning makes this transformation possible. It helps people to see how today's realities cannot be understood with yesterday's assumptions.

We must discard outmoded beliefs and attitudes and replace them with a clear view of the world as it is today. A school principal described the situation well when he said, "We are using educational methods of the 50's to prepare kids for a life in the 90's."

Burns has identified effective leaders for the restructuring of schools as transformational leaders.[54] Transformational leaders raise the behavior of followers to a higher moral level, which views the needs of the larger society. Following are some characteristics of effective leaders.[55]

1. *Effective leaders are data and future oriented.* They:
   - seek out data and information;
   - use individual experience and analytic skills to determine the implications and meanings of data;
   - seek out opportunities to compare perceptions and interpretations of data with others; and
   - project the meanings of data to knowledge of future trends.

2. *Effective leaders articulate visions of the future and suggest directions for change.* They:
   - encourage, assist, and guide collaborative planning efforts;
   - diagnose missing information or skills and seek to obtain the missing elements;
   - develop systematic programs that incorporate the goals of others;
   - mentor the development of others and seek to expand the capability of those they contact;
   - seek to build networks and relationships that can be mutually supportive; and
   - assist in identifying and solving potential and actual problems.
3. *Effective leaders are open to new ideas and experimentation.* They:
   - look for new approaches and ideas that may be applied to problem solving;
   - encourage risk taking even when the potential benefits may not be apparent; and
   - use failure as a source of learning rather than discouragement.
4. *Effective leaders provide hope and optimism for others.* They:
   - recognize others' growth and reinforce positive efforts to grow and learn;
   - recognize and articulate individual and organizational progress;
   - maintain realistic levels of hope and optimism; and
   - maintain continued communication and contact among diverse groups.

The need for leadership and change is apparent. The challenge is to develop human resources to meet these needs. History will not deal kindly with a nation of affluence that cannot meet the basic educational needs of its citizens. The stakes are high. We must be committed to using all our energies and tools such as strategic planning to build a new culture—an information society—if we are to give birth to the society waiting to be born.

# APPENDICES

# Appendix A

# Probable Directions for Educational Restructuring

The directions for restructuring provided below should help stimulate thinking about the ways in which districts may respond to the challenges facing education. The future of schools will, for the most part, be determined by leaders at the local level. The creativity and imagination of teachers, principals, superintendents, board members, and community members will establish the vision and direction for schools.

| Area | In an Industrial Society | In an Information Society |
| --- | --- | --- |
| *EDUCATION GOALS* | | |
| Cognitive Goals | Basic skills<br>Specific training<br>Right to read<br>Unicultural<br>Literacy as survival skill | Stronger higher-order<br>  skills<br>Generalizable skills<br>Right to excel<br>Global education<br>Many literacies, more<br>  than one language |
| Affective Goals | Large organization skills<br>Organization-dependent<br>Single-family orientation | Small-group skills<br>Independent,<br>  entrepreneurial<br>Support group orientation |
| Curriculum | Learning discipline skills<br>Standardized programs<br>Computer as separate<br>  vocational and literacy<br>  skill<br>Standardized programs | Interdisciplinary<br>  programs<br>Varied program options<br>Computer as learning tool<br>  in all programs<br>Varied program options |

| Area | In an Industrial Society | In an Information Society |
|---|---|---|
| Job Preparation | Single career preparation<br>Late skill development<br>Distinct vocational education programs | Multiple career preparation<br>Early skill development<br>Career/vocational education as integral part of educational community experience |

*DELIVERY SYSTEMS*

| Area | In an Industrial Society | In an Information Society |
|---|---|---|
| Changing Institutional Patterns | Single district system focus<br>Central office management<br>District single "product"<br>Top-down, insulated decision making<br>Superintendent-focused<br>Group instruction | More variety at building level<br>School-based management<br><br>Multiple options<br>Bottom-up, participative decision making<br>Principal-focused<br>Individualized instruction using technology |
| Changing Methodologies | Traditional instructional methods<br>Instructor/print-based systems<br>Computer-assisted instruction | Expanded instructional methods<br>Technology-assisted<br><br>Computer-cable-network-technologies |
| Expansion of Current Roles | Teacher as subject-matter expert<br><br><br><br>Teacher as standards setter<br>Teacher as deliverer of services<br><br>Principal as middle manager<br><br><br><br>Principal as central office conduit<br>Superintendent as preserver of tradition<br><br>Superintendent as educational leader<br><br>Student as recipient of knowledge | Teacher as manager/matter expert, facilitator of information and resources<br>Teacher as self-concept developer<br>Teacher as instructional/curriculum manager and planner<br>Principal as curriculum leader, staff developer, and neighborhood liaison as well as resource manager<br>Principal as program entrepreneur<br>Superintendent as future-oriented planner (manager of change)<br>Superintendent as community leader and resource developer<br>Student as extended "teacher" for staff and other students |

| Area | In an Industrial Society | In an Information Society |
|---|---|---|
| | School board as community servants | School board as directors of multi-million dollar businesses |
| New Roles | Textbook and software industries as suppliers and resource developers | Computer software development staff who supplement and tailor software to local needs |
| | Outside training consultants | Full-time institutional training staff |
| New Areas of Knowledge and Skills | Subject-matter knowledge Single discipline/areas expertise | Application of knowledge Interdisciplinary and learning processes expertise (learning how to learn) |
| | School administration Maintain tradition Print orientation | Program management Manage change Computer and computer peripherals orientation |

*EDUCATIONAL FINANCING*

| Area | In an Industrial Society | In an Information Society |
|---|---|---|
| Rationale and Scope | Individual development (schooling) Limited support for youth services Education as an expenditure | Economic development (forming human capital) Expanded support for total population services Education as an investment |
| Sources of Funds | Local taxes | Continued expansion of state funding and targeted funds |
| | Public tax funds | Extended business support and user fees |
| | Schools as limited revenue-producing institutions | Education-related functions and services to produce revenue |
| Distribution of Funds | Equalization of funds among districts | Greater emphasis on incentive, funding tied to district performance |
| | Undifferentiated salaries | Base salaries with incentives |
| | Single plan of employee benefits | Menu of employee benefits |

*COMMUNITY OUTREACH*

| Area | In an Industrial Society | In an Information Society |
|---|---|---|
| | Business as consumer of educational products | Business as participant and learning resource |
| | Formal hierarchies | Open communications networks |
| | Time-limited programs | Flexible, continuing education services |
| | Unitary systems | Learning community multiple options |

| Area | In an Industrial Society | In an Information Society |
|------|--------------------------|--------------------------|
|  | School as only learning site | School/home/business learning sites |
|  | School as education center | School as community center for varied ages and services |
|  | School district: youth-oriented | School district: lifelong learning-oriented |
|  | School as isolated educational institution | School as community service institution |
|  | Parent as advisor | Parent as participant |
|  | Parent as passive consumer | Parent as active consumer/decision maker |
|  | Student as passive consumer | Student as integral part of school and community and as peer instructor |

## Appendix B

# External Scanning Data Checklist

The following outlines a suggested list of categories of national and state data to be included in external environmental scanning. Because local situations vary, some data may not be relevant and other data may need to be added.

## Economic Data and Trends

**Economic Structure**

_____ Major income sources by economic sectors
_____ Small business and major corporate growth
_____ New business birth
_____ Growth projections
_____ Growth by sector: manufacturing, mining, construction, personal and business services, trade, finance, insurance, real estate, government, transportation, and public utilities
_____ Major income sources by sectors
_____ Retail sales
_____ Minority and female-owned businesses: trends and projections
_____ Impact of foreign investment and trade

**Employment**

_____ Labor force size and growth
_____ Work force growth projections
_____ Work force participation by age, sex, race/ethnicity and projections
_____ Occupational employment by managerial, professional, technical, sales, administrative support,

services, farming, fishing and forestry, precision production, operators, and laborers
_____ Occupational employment projections
_____ Occupational employment by sex and race/ethnicity and projections
_____ Employment by size of business establishment
_____ Blue collar vs. white collar and manufacturing vs. nonmanufacturing employment: trends and projections
_____ Unemployment by sector, sex, and race/ethnicity
_____ Work force continuing patterns
_____ Training programs for workers
_____ Part-time and temporary work force

## Income

_____ Per capita personal income
_____ Median household income
_____ Median family income
_____ Households and families under poverty level by age and race/ethnicity
_____ Income and poverty level projections
_____ Public assistance recipients
_____ Effective buying income
_____ Wage earnings by employment sector
_____ Income by age and race/ethnicity

# Demographic Data and Trends

## Population

_____ Population size and growth rate
_____ Size and growth projections
_____ Population density
_____ Population geographic distribution, diffusion, and mobility
_____ Birth rates
_____ Immigration

## Age

_____ Population by age and sex composition
_____ Population trends by age and sex
_____ Population by age and income

## Race/Ethnicity

_____ Size and growth rates of minority populations
_____ Age and sex composition of minority populations
_____ Projections for change in minority population
_____ Geographic distribution of minorities
_____ Income and poverty levels of minorities
_____ Educational levels of minorities
_____ Employment of minorities
_____ Single-parent families among minorities
_____ Foreign-born population trends
_____ Non-English-speaking populations

## Families and Households

_____ Number of households and projections
_____ Size of households and projections
_____ Number of families and projections
_____ Size of families and projections
_____ Marital status of individuals: trends and projections
_____ Single-parent families and projections
_____ Birth rate by age and race/ethnicity
_____ Number and size of families by race/ethnicity
_____ Marital status by race/ethnicity

## Sex Role Patterns

_____ Male and female population distribution by age
_____ Female labor force participation and projections
_____ Married female labor force participation
_____ Female heads of households and projections
_____ Female and male earnings and income
_____ Female poverty levels by age and race/ethnicity

# Social Data and Trends

## Health

_____ Life expectancy rates
_____ Infant mortality and causes
_____ Mortality rates and causes
_____ Abnormal births
_____ Births to teenagers
_____ Health problems of youth
_____ Mental illness by age and race/ethnicity
_____ Drug abuse
_____ Alcoholism

_____ Teen suicide
_____ Child abuse
_____ Nutritional problems
_____ Youth fitness

## Welfare

_____ Welfare recipients by size and projections
_____ Welfare recipients by category, age, and race/ethnicity
_____ Support services for welfare recipients (e.g., training, day care, and counseling programs)

## Housing

_____ Number of housing units and projections
_____ Age of housing
_____ Owner vs. renter housing
_____ Median percentage household income spent on housing
_____ Mean value of housing
_____ Seasonal vs. year-round units
_____ Average cost of housing with trends and projections
_____ Housing facilities available (heating equipment, sewage, telephone, etc.)
_____ Multi-family housing
_____ Occupancy and vacancy of housing
_____ Residential building permits, grants and dollar value

## Transportation

_____ Availability and use of public transportation
_____ Transportation to work and travel time to and from work
_____ Motor vehicle registration and car ownership

## Crime

_____ Violent and nonviolent reported crime rates and trends for adults and juveniles
_____ Crime rate projections
_____ Rates of imprisonment for adults and juveniles by sex and race/ethnicity

## Government

_____ State and local government budgets: income and expenditures
_____ Tax burden on individuals and projections

_____ Tax burden on corporations and projections
_____ Federal support to education
_____ State support to education
_____ Local tax support of education

## Education Data and Trends

_____ Educational levels of population
_____ Projections for educational attainment
_____ Illiteracy rates
_____ School enrollment trends by age, sex, and race/ethnicity
_____ School enrollment projections
_____ School dropout rates: trends and projections by age, sex, and race/ethnicity
_____ Perceptions of educational quality
_____ Achievement levels: trends by age, sex, and race/ethnicity
_____ Staff/student ratios
_____ Per pupil expenditures
_____ Use of technology
_____ Educational personnel numbers and projections of need
_____ Postsecondary education participation: trends and projections by sex and race/ethnicity

Other areas of data may be useful. The overall goal is to identify areas of relevance to education and training systems.

# Pattern Analysis: National Planning Assumptions

## Economic

- Greater international competition.
- Increase in foreign business ownership and investment in the United States.
- Offshore movement of U.S. jobs, markets, and industries.
- Moderate growth in U.S. Gross National Product (GNP).
- Growth in U.S. productivity.
- Possible continued cycles of recession.
- Varying economic conditions in geographic regions.
- Continued growth of small, entrepreneurial business.
- Growth of education and training to the major U.S. industry.
- Growth in income gap between the rich and poor in the United States.
- Growth in poverty of children in single-parent families.
- Slowdown in growth of U.S. labor force.
- Continued increase of women into the work force.
- Greater proportion of minorities in U.S. labor force.
- Increased competition for tax dollars.
- Increased use of robots in industrial and household settings.
- Growing problems of workers displaced by technological advances.

## Demographic and Social

- Slowdown in growth of U.S. population.
- Increase in rate of immigration, both legal and illegal.
- Continued aging of U.S. population.

- Greater proportional growth of minorities.
- Increase in number of households with decline in size of household.
- Growth of nonfamily households.
- Decline in number of children in U.S. families.
- Increase in single-parent families.
- Continued shifts in values.

## Political

- Continued concern about economic issues.
- Continued influence of single-issue groups.
- Growth in the influence of Baby Boom generation in U.S. politics.
- Continued trend toward decentralization of government to state and local levels.
- Growing influence of state legislators.

## Education

- Continuing concern with maintaining a work force with sufficient high-tech skills.
- Demand for increased quantity and quality of education.
- Demand for greater educational productivity.
- Increase in early childhood education.
- Increase in adult education and training.
- Expansion of expenditures for education, especially adult education.
- Growing demand for multiple options and alternatives.
- Shortage of qualified teachers.
- Higher levels of educational attainment.
- Increased concern about the achievement gap of disadvantaged children.
- Improved management systems in education.
- Expanded use of technology for instruction and management.

Adapted from the United Way of America,
*What Lies Ahead—A Mid-Decade View: An
Environmental Scan Report.* Alexandria,
Va.: United Way of America, 1985.

# Appendix D

# Internal Scanning Data Checklist

The following outlines a suggested list of categories and data to be included in an internal environmental or organizational capability scanning. All of the items listed may not be relevant, and other items may need to be added.

## Economic Data and Trends

**School finance**

_____ School budget by expenditures: trends and projections
_____ General tax support: local, state, and federal with trends and projections
_____ Special project funds: trends and projections
_____ Other sources of income

## Social/Demographic Data and Trends

**Students**

_____ K-12 enrollment: trends and projections
_____ Enrollment by grade and race/ethnicity
_____ Enrollment in special education programs
_____ Enrollment in alternative school programs by age, sex, and race/ethnicity
_____ Enrollment for adult education by programs and projections
_____ Pupil mobility within and outside district
_____ Pupil attendance patterns by age, sex, and race/ethnicity and trends
_____ Nonpromotions by age, sex, and race/ethnicity
_____ Exclusions, suspensions, and expulsions by reason, age, sex, and race/ethnicity and trends

_____ Dropouts by reason, age, sex, and race/ethnicity and trends

_____ Vandalism and other undesirable incidents

## Human Resources (Staff)

_____ Staff characteristics by roles

_____ Staff eligibility for retirement by role, sex, and race/ethnicity

_____ Staff development activities by role and participation

_____ Staff morale by role

_____ Staff absenteeism by role

## Pupil Personnel Services

_____ Attendance workers and services

_____ Guidance and counseling services and use

_____ Psychological services and use

_____ Social services and use

## Student Needs

_____ Students whose families receive Aid to Families with Dependent Children (AFDC) benefits and trends

_____ Students eligible for free or reduced-price lunch

_____ Students from single-parent families

_____ Students from limited- or non-English-speaking families

_____ Handicapped students by category

_____ Gifted students by program, age, sex, and race/ethnicity

_____ Teenage parents and available services

# · Educational Data and Trends

## Achievement

_____ Test results by school

_____ Test results by age, sex, and race/ethnicity and trends

_____ Scholarships, recognition, and awards

_____ Postsecondary participation by sex and race/ethnicity and trends

## Curriculum

_____ Elementary offerings and trends

_____ Middle and junior high offerings and trends

_____ High school offerings and trends

_____ Special education offerings and trends
_____ Alternative or magnet programs and trends
_____ Studies and curriculum reviews
_____ Vocational education offerings and trends
_____ Early childhood education offerings and trends
_____ School libraries and resource centers
_____ Community programs or resources

## Organization and Management

_____ Board of education role and composition
_____ Administrative organization
_____ District or building structure
_____ Planning processes in operation
_____ Supervision and monitoring activities

## Support Services

_____ Building services based on student needs and trends
_____ Building programs
_____ School closings
_____ School maintenance and upkeep status
_____ Energy conservation programs
_____ Student transportation services
_____ Food services
_____ Central purchasing
_____ Materials, supplies, and publications
_____ Equipment acquisitions and needs
_____ Security services and needs

# Technology Data and Trends

## Technology Plans

_____ Needs assessment for technology uses
_____ Goals for technology plans
_____ Current efforts in using technology
_____ Problems in technology usage
_____ Continuing and future needs

# Political and Public Relations Data and Trends

## Labor, Legal, and Legislative Affairs

_____ Labor union relations and trends
_____ Legal issues and concerns

_____ Legislative issues (local, state, and federal) that affect the district

## Community Relations

_____ Parent and school relations and programs
_____ School and community relations and programs
_____ School and business relations and programs
_____ Postsecondary institutions relations and programs
_____ Media relations and programs

## Governance

_____ Board and community relations
_____ School and district advisory groups

# Appendix E

# Example of Data Analysis

| Form of Information | Description | Environmental Monitoring |
|---|---|---|
| Raw Data | Numerical and graphic data, data from census reports, survey data. | Census data indicate greater labor force participation by mothers of young children. |
| Research Reports | Studies of Headstart and other early childhood education programs. | Studies report the value of early childhood education for disadvantaged children. |
| Trends and Projections | Statements about social, political, economic, or technological events that can be measured over time. | Labor force participation by mothers of preschoolers is increasing. This trend will continue throughout the decade. |
| | | There is an increased demand for day-care programs for children, especially developmental programs. |
| | | Disadvantaged children continue to achieve at lower levels. |
| Scenario Development | Likely outcomes of a decision to provide or extend early childhood education. | Positive response, successful program may be self-supporting. |
| | | Inadequate response, program may need to be discontinued after a period of time. |
| | | Positive response, inadequate program planning and staff capability. |
| | | Demonstration or limited program to develop |

| Form of Information | Description | Environmental Monitoring |
| --- | --- | --- |
| | | organizational capability before major expansion. |
| Decision Points | Evaluation of possible scenarios and discussion of alternative responses. | Education seems to make a positive difference. |
| Assumptions | Statements of trends and projections that are accepted as highly probable and assumed to hold true for the planning task. | We assume that greater proportions of working mothers will continue to participate in the work force. |
| Implications | Statements of what trends mean. | There will be a growing need for day-care and early childhood education programs. |
| Issues | Synthesis of implications into questions for the organization. | Should the school district provide or extend early childhood education programs? |
| | | How could such expansion be supported financially? |
| | | Does the district have space for programs? |
| Critical Issue | Most critical concerns for the organization. | Is there adequate need and support for such services? |

# NOTES

1. John Naisbitt, speech to the California Association of School Administrators, November 1983.

2. Futures Research Division, Security Pacific Bank as reported by the United Way of America in *What Lies Ahead—A Mid-Decade View: An Environmental Scan Report* (Alexandria, Va.: United Way of America, 1985), 27.

3. Marc Uri Porat, *The Information Economy: Definition and Measurement* (Washington, D.C.: U.S. Department of Commerce, 1977).

4. U.S. Department of Labor as reported in *Changing Channels: A Guide to Functional Literacy for the Automated Workplace* ed. Nancy Faires Conklin and Stephen Reder (Portland: Northwest Regional Educational Laboratory, 1985), 3.

5. Paul A. Strassmann, *Information Payoff: The Transformation of Work in the Electronic Age* (New York: The Free Press, 1985), 197–198.

6. Office of Technology Assessment, United States Congress, *Automation and the Workplace: Selected Labor, Education and Training Issues* (Washington, D.C.: Office of Technology Assessment, 1983), 13.

7. Ibid., 14–15.

8. Bryna Shore Fraser, *(Re)Training Adults for New Office and Business Technologies* (Knoxville: Office for Research in High Technology Education, The University of Tennessee, 1984), 9.

9. Strassmann, *Information Payoff*, 199.

10. David Pearce Snyder, "Demographic, Economic and Social Trends and Developments that Will Shape the Organizational Operating Environment During the 1980s" (unpublished paper).

11. Robert R. Carkhuff, *Human Processing and Human Productivity* (Amherst: Human Resource Development Press, 1986), 143.

12. National Research Council of the National Academy of Sciences, *Outlook for Science and Technology: The Next Five Years* (San Francisco: W. H. Freeman and Company, 1982), 1.

13. Ibid., 3.

14. University of Michigan, Center for Human Growth and Development, 1984.

15. United Way of America, *What Lies Ahead—A Mid-Decade View: An Environmental Scan Report* (Alexandria, Va.: United Way of America, 1985), 24.

16. Ibid., 24.

17. Mark Tucker, *A Nation Prepared: Teachers for the 21st Century* (Carnegie Forum on Education and the Economy, Task Force on Teaching as a Profession, May 1986).

18. United Way of America, *What Lies Ahead*, 26.

19. U.S. Bureau of the Census (Washington D.C.: U.S. Department of Commerce, 1980).

20. United Way of America, *What Lies Ahead*, 34–35.

21. Ibid., 34.

22. Ibid.

23. Ibid.

24. Ibid., 34–35.

25. Harold Hodgkinson, *All In One System: Demographics of Education Kindergarten Through Graduate School* (Washington, D.C.: Institute for Educational Leadership, June 1985), 13.

26. David Pearce Snyder, "Demographic, Economic and Social Trends."

27. "The Patterns in Our Social Fabric Are Changing: Here They Come, Ready or Not," *Education Week*, 14 May 1986, 16.

28. Ibid.

29. Harold Hodgkinson, *All In One System*, 16.

30. *Education Week*, "Patterns in Our Social Fabric."

31. Ibid., 18.

32. Ibid., 16.

33. Education Commission of the States, *Reconnecting Youth: The Next Stage of Reform* (Denver: Education Commission of the States, October 1985).

34. *Education Week*, "Patterns in Our Social Fabric," 22.

35. Ibid., 24.

36. Ibid., 22.

37. Lenore Wertzman, *Divorce Revolution: The Unintended Consequences for Women and Children* (New York: Macmillan, 1985).

38. Harold Hodgkinson, *All in One System*, 3.

39. *Education Week*, "Patterns in Our Social Fabric," 22.

40. Ibid.

41. Ibid.

42. U.S. Bureau of the Census, *Social Indicators III* (Washington, D.C.: U.S. Department of Commerce, 1980).

43. *Education Week*, "Patterns in Our Social Fabric," 25.

44. Andrew Stein, "Children of Poverty: Crisis in New York, *New York Times Magazine*, 8 June 1986.

45. *Education Week*, "Patterns in Our Social Fabric," 27.

46. U.S. Bureau of the Census as reported in *Education Week*, "Patterns in Our Social Fabric," 27.

47. David Weikart et al., *Changed Lives* (Ypsilanti, Mich.: High/Scope Educational Research Foundation, 1984).

48. Karl L. Alexander and Aaron M. Pallas, *An Evaluation of the "New Basics"* (Baltimore: Center for Social Organization of Schools, The Johns Hopkins University, 1983).

49. Edward L. McDill, Gary Natriello, and Aaron M. Pallas, *Raising Standards and Retaining Students: The Impact of the Reform Recommendations on Potential Dropouts* (Baltimore: Center for Social Organization of Schools, The Johns Hopkins University, 1985).

50. Thomas J. Peters and Robert H. Waterman, Jr., *In Search of Excellence* (Cambridge: Harper and Row, 1982), 318–325.

51. Rosabeth Kanter, *The Change Masters* (New York: Simon and Schuster, 1983), 28–30.

52. Peters and Waterman, *In Search of Excellence.*

53. James Murphy and Phillip Hallinger, "The Superintendent as Instructional Leader: Findings from Effective School Districts" (paper presented at American Educational Research Association meeting, San Francisco, April 1986).

54. James MacGregor Burns, *Leadership* (New York: Harper and Row, 1978).

55. Framework developed by Shirley D. McCune. Examples of characteristics from informal paper developed by Harold Hodgkinson.

# BIBLIOGRAPHY

Albert, Kenneth, ed. *The Strategic Management Handbook*. New York: McGraw-Hill, 1983.

Arthur Andersen & Company. "Guide to Public Sector Strategic Planning." Chicago-World Headquarters, 69 W. Washington, Chicago, IL 60602.

Brandt, Steven. *Strategic Planning in Emerging Companies*. Reading, Pa.: Addison-Wesley Publishing Company, 1984.

Buhler-Miko, Marina. *A Trustee's Guide to Strategic Planning*. Higher Education Strategic Planning Institute, One Dupont Circle, Washington, DC 20036, 1985.

Cooper, Harry. *Strategic Planning in Education: A Guide for Policymakers*. Alexandria, Va.: National Association of State Boards of Education, 1985.

Cope, Robert. "A Contextual Model to Encompass the Strategic Planning Concept: Introducing a Newer Paradigm." *Planning for Higher Education 13, 3* (Spring 1985): 13–20.

Cope, Robert. *Strategic Policy Planning*. Littleton, Colo.: Ireland Educational Corporation, 1978.

Groff, Warren. "Strategic Planning for the 'Third Wave'." Paper presented at a Futurists International Meeting, Washington D.C. Spring 1983. (ERIC #ED 233 651).

Lilly, Edward. "Boards of Education and System-wide Strategic Planning." ERIC #248 613.

Masuda, Yoneji. *The Information Society as Post-Industrial Society*, Tokyo, Japan: Society for the Information Society, 1980.

McCune, Shirley D., et al. "Strategic Planning." *Learning Trends 1, 7* (February 1984).

Morrison, James. "Futures Research and Strategic Planning Process: Implications for Long Range Planning." ERIC #245 587.

Paine, Frank, and Carl Anderson. *Strategic Management*. New York: CBS College Publishing, 1983.

Perelman, Lewis J. "The Value of Business Intelligence." Strategic Performance Services, P.O. Box 5500, McLean, VA 22103, 1982.

Phi Delta Kappa Commission on Schooling for the 21st Century. *Handbook for Conducting Future Studies in Education*. Bloomington, Ind.: Phi Delta Kappa, 1984.

Pfeiffer, J. William, Leonard D. Goodstein, and Timothy M. Nolan. *Understanding Applied Strategic Planning: A Manager's Guide*. University Associates, Inc., 8517 Production Ave., San Diego, CA 92121, 1985.

Public Technology, Inc. *Alliances for Strategic Action*. Washington D.C.: Public Technology, Inc., 1983.

Rothschild, William. *Putting it All Together: A Guide to Strategic Thinking*. American Management Associates, 1976.

Steiner, George A. "Strategic Managerial Planning." Graduate School of Management, UCLA.

Steiner, George A. *Strategic Planning: What Every Manager Must Know*. New York: The Free Press, 1979.

Tregoe, Benjamin B., and John W. Zimmerman. *Top Management Strategy*. New York: Simon & Schuster, Inc., 1980.

United Way of America. *Strategic Management and United Way—A Guideline Series*. Strategic Planning Division, 701 North Fairfax St., Alexandria, VA 22314-2045, 1985. Booklets in the series include:
1. *Strategic Management and United Way*. An overview of the strategic process, including process steps, benefits, costs, and how to get started.
2. *Environmental Analysis*. How to do environmental analysis. Discusses use of environmental scanning, environmental monitoring, and scenario development to define external threats to and opportunities for the organization.
3. *Organizational Assessment*. How to assess the organization's internal strengths and weaknesses and its competitive position by looking at both resources and operations. Reviews methods for organizational assessment, including comparative analysis, analysis of performance history, self-assessment, surveys, interviews, and focus groups.
4. *Strategic Direction*. How to use data from environmental analysis and organizational assessment to review the mission, set objectives, and identify strategic issues critical to the organization.
5. *Strategic Plan*. How to document specific courses of action and define how the organization is going to fulfill its mission and objectives in dealing with critical issues.
6. *Implementation*. How to organize and motivate people to carry out a strategic plan.
7. *Performance Evaluation*. How to compare actual results with anticipated or desired results of the strategic process. How to keep implementation on target by adjusting strategies, resources, and timing.
8. *Case Studies*. This volume will follow publication of booklets 1–7 and will review the experiences of pilot United Ways in using the strategic management process.

United Way of America. *What Lies Ahead—A Mid-Decade View: An Environmental Scan Report*. Alexandria, Va.: United Way of America, 1985.

Vaill, Peter. "Strategic Planning for Managers." *National Training Lab Managers' Handbook*.